SMALL STEPS

LOUIS SACHAR

Long tail Books

SMALL STEPS

This English edition was published by Longtail Books in 2012 by arrangement with Louis Sachar c/o Trident Media Group, LLC, New York through KCC(Korea Copyright Center Inc.), Seoul.

ISBN 979-11-91343-92-2 14740

Longtail Books

To Laura and Nancy,
for all you taught me

1

Once again Armpit was holding a **shovel**, only now he was getting paid for it, seven dollars and sixty-five cents an hour. He worked for Raincreek **Irrigation** and **Landscaping**. He was in the **process** of digging a **trench** along the side yard of a house that belonged to the **mayor** of Austin, a woman with the **unusual** name of Cherry Lane. As his shovel knifed through the **dirt**, he carefully kept the **sod intact** so that it could be **replace**d later. His shovel was short and had a **rectangular blade**, unlike the five-foot★ shovels with pointed blades he had used when he was at Camp Green Lake **Juvenile Correct**ional **Facility**.

Beads of **perspiration** rolled out from under his red RAINCREEK cap. His shirt was **drench**ed in **sweat**. Yet none of this **had anything to do with** how he got his name.

During his first week at Camp Green Lake, close to three

★ feet 길이의 단위 피트. 1피트는 30.48센티미터이다. 숫자와 연결하여 쓸 때에는 하이픈을 넣고 단수형 foot으로 쓴다. five-foot는 약 152센티미터이다.

years before, a **scorpion** had **stung** him on the arm, and the pain had traveled upward and settled in his **armpit**. It had felt like there was a hot needle **twist**ing around inside him. He'd made the mistake of **complain**ing about how much his armpit hurt. The pain **eventually** went away, but the name **stuck**.

"Theodore!" called his boss, Jack Dunlevy, a white man in his late thirties. "There's someone who would like to meet you."

Armpit stopped digging as his boss and a woman **approach**ed. The woman wore blue jeans and a loose-fitting white shirt. Her long silver hair was pulled back in a **ponytail**. Austin had a **reputation** for being a little **weird**, and the mayor fit right in.

"This is Theodore Johnson," said his boss.

Cherry Lane **extend**ed her hand. "How ya doin',★ Theodore?"

Armpit **stood** a head taller than the mayor. He had **broad** shoulders and thick **muscular** arms. At one time in his life he had been a little **overweight**, but all his digging and sweating had long since burned away any **excess** fat.

"Just fine," he said as he wiped his dirty hand on his shorts. "Sorry, I'm kind of **sweaty**."

"That's all right," the mayor said, and shook his hand.

Afraid of his own strength, Armpit tried not to **grip** the **elder**ly woman's hand too hard, and **was** a little **taken aback** by the **firm**ness of her handshake.

★ **How ya doin'** How are you doing?

"I read all about the **terrible** things that went on at Camp Green Lake," she told him. "I want you to know that I **admire** you for **get**ting **through** it and turning your life around."

Armpit wasn't sure what to say. "I admire what you've done for Austin."

He really had no idea what she'd done for the city. He knew she was supposed to be a strong **environmentalist**, but he'd heard his dad complain on several **occasion**s that the "tree-huggers,★" only seemed to care about west Austin, an area well known for its **rolling** hills, nature **preserve**s, and hike and bike **trail**s. Most African Americans,✳ including Armpit's family, lived in the **flatland**s of east Austin.

A **mosquito buzz**ed by his ear, and he **swat**ted at it. At least there hadn't been mosquitoes at Green Lake. It was too dry.

He had been sent to Camp Green Lake because of a **bucket** of popcorn. He had been trying to **ease** his way along a **row** of seats at the movies. He was only fourteen at the time, and was making his way past a couple of high school **senior**s when one of them **stuck out** his foot. They **yell**ed at him for **spill**ing popcorn on them, and he demanded that they pay for the popcorn, and by the time it was all over, the two older boys were in the hospital, and he was on his way to Camp Green Lake Juvenile Correctional Facility.

The name Green Lake was a **cruel** joke. He spent fourteen

★ **tree-huggers** 급진적인 환경 보호 운동가.

✳ **African American** 아프리카계 미국인.

months in a dried-up lake **bed**, where he did nothing except dig holes. Later, when he **applied** for a job at Raincreek, Jack Dunlevy warned him the job would require a **fair** bit of digging. Armpit just smiled and said, "No sweat.★"

After leaving Camp Green Lake, he first spent six months at a halfway house✻ in San Antonio, where he attended school and received **counsel**ing. There were sixteen boys at the halfway house. The counselor there told them that the **recidivism** rate for African American boys was seventy-three percent. That meant, according to the **statistics**, that eleven or twelve of them would be **arrest**ed again before they turned eighteen. The counselor said the rate was even higher if you didn't finish high school.

"If you think life was unfair before you went to **prison**," she told Armpit, "it's going to be twice as bad when you go back. People are going to expect the worst from you, and will treat you that way."

She said his life would be like walking **upstream** in a **rush**ing river. The secret was to take small steps and just keep moving forward. If he tried to take too big a step, the **current** would **knock** him **off** his feet and carry him back **downstream**.

Upon returning to Austin, he set five goals for himself. Five small steps. 1. **Graduate** from high school. 2. Get a job. 3. Save his money. 4. Avoid situations that might turn **violent**. And 5.

★ no sweat 땀이 없다, 즉 힘들이지 않고 할 수 있다는 뜻.
✻ halfway house 교도소 출소자나 정신 병원 퇴원 환자 등을 위한 사회 복귀 훈련 시설.

Lose the name Armpit.

He picked up his shovel and went back to his trench.

Jack Dunlevy always brought a radio to the work **site**, and it was now playing a song by Kaira DeLeon.

I'm gonna take you for a ride,
And we're gonna have some fun!

The mayor, who had started to walk away, came hurrying back. "Oh, I love this song!" she **exclaim**ed.

I'm gonna take you for a ride,
Ooh, and we're gonna have some fun!

Cherry Lane raised her arms in the air as she **wiggle**d to the music. Armpit tried not to laugh. At least there was music. There had been no radios to listen to when he was digging holes at Camp Green Lake.

I'm gonna take you someplace
you never been before,
And you'll never be the same again!

2

A **rust**ed Honda Civic★ drove noisily down the street and parked across from the **mayor**'s house. Armpit had finished digging his **trench** and was **attach**ing PVC✶ pipe. The mayor had gone back inside.

The driver-side door had been **bash**ed in, and it would have cost more to fix than the car was **worth**. The driver had to work his way over the **stick shift**❋ and then **exit** on the **passenger** side.

The **personalized license** plate read: X RAY.

"Armpit!" X-Ray shouted as he crossed the street. "Armpit!"

The guys at work didn't know him by that name, but if he didn't say something X-Ray would just keep on shouting. Better

---

★ Honda Civic 혼다(Honda)사에서 나오는 차.
✶ PVC (= polyvinyl chloride) 폴리염화비닐. PVC 파이프는 내약품성이 우수하여 부식이나 침식의 염려가 없이 장기간 사용할 수 있어 배수관, 하수관 등으로 사용된다.
❋ stick shift 자동차의 수동 변속기.

to answer and **shut him up**.

"Hey," he called back.

"Man, you're really **sweat**ing," X-Ray said as he came near.

"Yeah, well, you'd sweat too if you were digging."

"I've already dug enough **dirt** to **last** one **lifetime**," said X-Ray.

They had met each other at Camp Green Lake.

"Look, don't call me Armpit around other people, all right?" Armpit said.

"But that's your name, dawg.★ You should never be **ashamed** of who you are."

X-Ray had the kind of smile that kept you from hating him no matter how **annoy**ing he was. He was **skinny** and wore glasses, which were now covered with clip-on **shade**s.✱

He picked up Armpit's **shovel**. "Different shape."

"Yeah, it's for digging trenches, not holes."

X-Ray studied it awhile. "Seems like it would be harder to dig with. No **leverage**." He let it drop. "So you must be making a ton of money."

Armpit **shrug**ged. "I'm doing all right."

"A ton of money," X-Ray repeated.

Armpit felt uncomfortable talking about money with X-Ray.

"So really, how much you got saved up so far?"

"I don't know. Not that much."

★ **dawg** 미국 흑인들이 친한 사람을 부를 때 쓰는 말.

✱ **clip-on shades** 투명한 일반 안경에 끼었다 뺐다 하는 선글라스 렌즈.

He knew exactly how much he had. Eight hundred and fifty-seven dollars. He hoped to break a thousand with his next **paycheck**.

"Got to be at least a thousand," said X-Ray. "You've been working for three months."

"Just part-time."

Besides working, Armpit was also taking two classes in summer school. He had to **make up for** all the schooling he'd missed while at Green Lake.

"And they take out for **taxes** and **stuff**, so really I don't take home all that much."

"Eight hundred?"

"I don't know, maybe."

"The reason I'm asking," X-Ray said, "the reason I'm asking is I got a business **proposition** for you. How would you like to double your money in less than two weeks?"

Armpit smiled as he shook his head. "I don't think so."

"I just need six hundred dollars. Double your money, **guaranteed**. And I won't be taking out any taxes."

"Look, things are going all right for me right now, and I just want to **keep it** all **cool**."

"Don't you even want to **hear** me **out**?"

"Not really."

"It's not against the law," X-Ray **assured** him. "I checked."

"Yeah, you didn't think selling little bags of parsley★ for

★ **parsley** 파슬리. 장식이나 맛을 낼 때 쓰는 향신료의 일종.

fifty dollars an ounce,★ was against the law either."

"Hey, it's not my fault what people *think* they're buying. How is that my fault? Am I supposed to be a mind reader?"

X-Ray had been sent to Camp Green Lake for selling bags of dried parsley and oregano✵ to customers who thought they were buying marijuana.❋ That was also why his family had to move from Lubbock to Austin shortly after he was **released**.

"Look, I just don't want to do anything that might **screw** things **up**," Armpit said.

"That's what you think? That I came here to screw things up? Man, I'm **offer**ing you an **opportunity**. An opportunity. If the Wright brothers✳ came to you, you would have told them it's impossible to fly."

"*The Wright brothers?*" asked Armpit. "What **century** are you living in?"

"I just don't **get it**," said X-Ray. "I don't get it. I offer my best friend an opportunity to double his money, and he won't even listen to my idea."

"All right, tell me your idea."

"Forget it. If you're not interested I'll find somebody else."

"Tell me your idea." He actually was beginning to get just a little bit **curious**.

"What's the point?" asked X-Ray. "If you're not going to even

---

★ **ounce** 무게의 단위 온스. 1온스는 28.35그램이다.

✵ **oregano** 오레가노. 허브의 일종.

❋ **marijuana** 마리화나. 대마초라고도 하며, 마약의 한 종류이다.

✳ **Wright brothers** 라이트 형제. 비행기 제작자이자 항공계를 개척한 사람들이다.

listen . . ."

"All right, I'm listening," said Armpit.

X-Ray smiled. "Just two words." He **paused for effect**. "Kaira DeLeon."

It was eleven-thirty in Austin, but it was an hour later in Atlanta, where Kaira DeLeon, a seventeen-year-old African American girl, was just waking up. Her face pressed against **Pillow**, which was, in fact, a pillow. There wasn't much **oomph** left in the **stuffing**, and the **edge**s were **fray**ed. The picture of the bear with a balloon, which had once been brightly colored, had **fade**d so much it was hardly **visible**.

Kaira **groggily** climbed out of bed. She wore **boxer shorts** and was unbuttoning her **pajama** top as she made her way to what she thought was the bathroom. She opened the door, then **shriek**ed. A thirty-year-old white guy, sitting on a **couch**, stared back at her. She **clutch**ed the two halves of her pajama top together and **slam**med the door.

The door **bounce**d back open.

"**Doofus**!" Kaira shouted at the man, then closed the door again, making sure it **latch**ed this time. "Can't a person have some **privacy** around here!" she screamed, then made her way to the bathroom, which was on the **opposite** side of her bed.

Over the last three and a half weeks she'd been in nineteen different hotel **suite**s, each with no fewer than three rooms, and one with six. So really, it was no wonder she went through the wrong door. She didn't even remember what city she was in.

She **suspect**ed that Polly, her **psychiatrist**, would tell her she had done that on **purpose**; something about wanting to show her body to her bodyguard. Maybe she **was better off** not telling Polly about it. Everything she said in her **therapy session**s was supposed to be **confidential**, but Kaira suspected that Polly, like a **parrot**, repeated everything to El Genius.

She had no privacy—not in her hotel room, not even in her own thoughts.

The problem was that, except for Polly, there wasn't anybody on the tour she could talk to. Certainly not her mother. And not her doofus bodyguard. The guys in her band were all at least forty years old, and treated her like she was a **snot**-nosed little kid. The backup singers* were in their late twenties, but they seemed to **resent** her being the center of attention.

The only time she felt at peace was when she was singing. Then it was just her and the song and everybody else just disappeared.

Her concert tour would take her to a total of fifty-four cities, so she wasn't even half done yet. She was now on the southern **swing**. From Atlanta they'd be going to Jacksonville, then Miami, Birmingham, Memphis, Nashville, Little Rock, and Baton Rouge, and on to Texas: Houston, Austin, and Dallas. **Original**ly the tour was supposed to include San Antonio instead of Austin, but that was changed at the last minute **due**

★ **backup singers** 가수의 뒤를 받쳐서 화음을 넣어주는 가수들.
✱ **monster truck rally** 소형 오픈 트럭을 개조해 만든 차로 하는 경주.

to a monster truck **rally*** at the Alamodome—not that Kaira cared, or even knew about the change.

Other people took care of things like that. Other people took care of everything. Kaira had **accidental**ly left Pillow behind in New Haven, and Aileen, the tour's travel **coordinator**, took a flight back to Connecticut and **personal**ly searched the hotel **laundry** until she found it.

ᔓ

Kaira **emerge**d from the bathroom thirty minutes later wearing a hotel **robe**. She called room service and ordered a glass of orange juice, pancakes, a cappuccino,* and French fries. It would have to last her until the concert. If she tried to eat before the concert she'd **puke**. After a concert she usually had a bowl of ice cream.

She got dressed, then stepped back out to the sitting area. Fred, her doofus bodyguard, was still there, **going through** her mail.

"As soon as I turn eighteen, you're going to be the second person I **fire**."

Fred didn't even look up. It wasn't the first time he'd heard it.

The television was on CNN. Kaira changed the **station** to the Cartoon Network.

The first person she'd fire would be El Genius. He was her business manager and **agent**, and also happened to be married

---

★ **cappuccino** 카푸치노. 스팀 우유 거품을 에스프레소 위에 얹어 만든 커피.

to her mother. They had gotten married shortly before the tour. His real name was Jerome Paisley, but he actually wanted people to call him El Genius. No matter how hard Kaira tried to sound **sarcastic** when she used that name, he always took it as a **compliment**.

Her father had been killed in Iraq. His name was John Spears. Kaira's real name was Kathy Spears, but there was already a famous singer with that last name.

El Genius had **come up with** the name Kaira DeLeon.

"You mean like Ponce de León?★" Kaira had asked him.

"Who?"

Some **genius**.

Kaira explained to *the genius* who Ponce de León was, which was why her first CD was **titled** ***The Fountain of Youth***. El Genius thought it looked **classy** for DeLeon to be spelled as one word, with a **capital** letter in the middle.

Kaira had learned all about Ponce de León when she was in fourth grade and living at the Pensacola Naval Air Station. She had to learn the history of Florida. By year's end she was living at Fort Myer, where they'd been studying the history of Virginia all year. She had never spent an **entire** school year in the same place.

"So, anything from Billy Boy?" she asked Fred.

Fred shook his head.

"Aw, too bad," Kaira said. "He writes such **charm**ing letters."

★ **Ponce de León** 폰세데레온. 15세기 스페인의 탐험가.

"It's not funny," said Fred.

"I think it's **hilarious**," said Kaira. She sang, "*Oh, where have you been, Billy Boy, Billy Boy? Oh, where have you been, charming Billy?*"

Billy Boy had sent her four letters so far. He told her he thought she was lovely, she sang like a bird, and someday he would kill her.

El Genius **hire**d Fred after the first letter. Kaira wouldn't have been surprised if El Genius had actually written the letters, to scare her into staying **confine**d to her hotel room. He was such a control **freak**. She was sure Fred told him everything she did.

"You got another marriage **proposal**," Fred said.

"White or black?"

A photograph had been sent with the letter. Fred looked at it. "White," he said.

"What is it with you guys?" asked Kaira.

It was her seventh proposal, and every one had been from a white man.

Fred carefully put the letter and the photograph in a **plastic bag**.

"What are you doing that for?"

"FBI.★"

"He said he wanted to marry me, not kill me," Kaira **point**ed **out**.

★ FBI (= Federal Bureau of Investigation) (미국) 연방 수사국.

"For some people, it's the same thing," said Fred.

Kaira **glanced** at him, surprised. The Doofus had actually said something kind of **profound**.

"Let me see what he looks like?"

Fred handed her the plastic bag.

Kaira laughed when she saw the picture. "He looks like you!" The photograph was that of a very **muscular** man wearing no shirt. The only difference between him and Fred was that his hair was long and **wavy**, while Fred had a buzz cut.★

"You ought to grow your hair out," Kaira told him as she handed the plastic bag back to him.

Seven marriage proposals, and she'd never had a boyfriend.

"Okay, here's the deal," said X-Ray. "Here's the deal. They just added Austin to her tour because of some kind of **screwup** in San Antonio. Tickets go on sale day after tomorrow. Fifty-five dollars a pop.✳"

"Fifty-five dollars for just one ticket? I don't think so."

"In Philadelphia two front-**row** seats sold for seven hundred fifty dollars. Each."

Armpit couldn't believe it. "Seven hundred and fifty—"

"Each," X-Ray repeated.

"She's got a nice voice," said Armpit. "Kind of **sassy**, and

★ **buzz cut** 아주 짧게 깎은 머리.
✳ **pop** (속어) 1개, 1회. 여기서는 티켓 한 장에 55달러라는 말이다.

playful, you know? You can always tell it's her."

X-Ray looked at him like he was crazy. "I don't want a **critique**! I want six hundred dollars." He spoke as if to somebody else. "He gives me a critique. Now he's a **critic**."

"Well, if I didn't think she could sing, I wouldn't give you six hundred dollars."

"So you're going to give me the money?"

He was **consider**ing it.

"See, here's the deal," X-Ray explained. "They only let you buy six tickets. So together we can buy twelve. Six hundred and sixty dollars. I've already got sixty, so I just need the rest from you. You won't have to do a thing. I'll do all the work. Then we'll **split** the **profits**."

Armpit slowly **exhaled**. "Six hundred dollars," he said.

"You'll make that back on one ticket," said X-Ray.

"No one's going to pay six hundred dollars for a ticket."

"They paid seven hundred and fifty in Philadelphia."

Armpit picked up his shovel and began filling in the dirt around the pipe.

"Okay, let's say we only sell the tickets for two hundred," said X-Ray. "After three tickets you get your money back. I won't get any of that. Then I get my sixty back out of the next ticket, and we split the rest right down the middle. So really there's no **risk** to you at all. You know we can sell three tickets."

Armpit **replaced** the **sod**, **stomp**ing it down with his boot.

"Think of it this way. It's like someone is offering to pay you to stand in line for him. What if your boss says to you, he says, 'Armpit, instead of digging today, I want you to stand in line for me, and I'll pay you a thousand **bucks** to do it.' Wouldn't you do it?"

"Of course."

"Same thing!" X-Ray said. "Some **dudes** are going to pay us a thousand bucks to stand in line for them. We just don't know who they are yet. See, you got to **think outside the box**."

A **siren blared** over the radio.

"Oh! Oh!" X-Ray **exclaimed** as he **fumbled** for the cell phone attached to his belt.

The siren noise had been made by an **electric** guitar, which slowly **wound down** and **transformed** into a **flurry** of **notes** and **chords**. It was the **intro** to Kaira DeLeon's biggest hit.

I hear a w-w-warning sound
Every time you c-c-come around.
Should you ch-chance to glance at me,
***Threatens** my **security**.*

"C'mon, c'mon," X-Ray said into his phone.

Red Alert!★
My hands are sh-sh-shakin'.
*Red Alert! **Stomach's achin'**.*

★ **red alert** 적색 경보. 미국의 경계상황 등급은 '녹색(low)'부터 시작해서 '청색(guarded)' '황색(elevated)' '주황색(high)' '적색(severe)' 5단계로 구성되며, red alert는 가장 심각한 위험을 말한다.

Red Alert!
The earth beneath my f-f-feet is ***quakin'****.*

"Yeah—no, wait!" X-Ray said into the phone. "Just wait a sec—★"

He **scowl**ed as he returned his phone to his belt. "Sixth," he **gripe**d. "Can you believe it? Sixth! Fifth caller gets two free tickets. Man, I hate this phone. The speed **dial**✱ is too slow. How you supposed to **compete** with those rich white kids who have newer phones?"

"Too bad," said Armpit. "That woulda been❋ at least another four hundred for us,"

X-Ray said. "For us?"

"Sure man, we're partners now, right?"

Armpit considered this question seriously. If he gave the money to X-Ray, at least he'd still have two hundred and fifty-seven dollars left.

"Right?" X-Ray asked again.

Red Alert!
My head is filled with a s-s-siren sound!
Red Alert!
All systems are ***shutting*** *d-d-d-d-****down!***

★ sec 'second(초)'의 줄임말.
✱ speed dial 전화의 단축 다이얼번호.
❋ woulda been would have been.

"Yeah, we're partners," Armpit agreed.

X-Ray **pat**ted him on the shoulder. "You won't regret it."

He already did.

3

Interstate 35* goes from the Mexican **border** all the way up to Lake Superior,* and some of the heaviest **traffic** is along the two-hundred-fifty-mile **stretch** between San Antonio and Dallas. The steady **flow** of cars and trucks divides the city of Austin in half, not just **geographical**ly, but also **economic**ally, and to some **extent**, **racial**ly.

Armpit's home was in east Austin. The house was a duplex,* with two **identical** front doors that faced each other across a wide front **porch**, 141A and 141B. Armpit's family lived in 141B. It was just him and his parents. He had an older sister who was married and lived in Houston, and an older brother **serving** eight to ten at Huntsville.

★ **Interstate 35** interstate는 미국의 각 주(州) 사이에 놓인 고속도로를 말한다. Interstate 35는 주간 고속도로 35번이다.

✳ **Lake Superior** 슈피리어호(湖). 미국 5대호의 하나로, 세계 최대의 담수호이다.

❋ **duplex** (= duplex apartment) 2세대용 주택.

A white woman and her ten-year-old daughter, Ginny McDonald, **occupied** the other half of the house.

"S-s-six hun-did d-dollahs?" said Ginny. She was small for her age, with **skinny** arms and legs. She wore glasses that were so thick it was a wonder they could **stay up** on her tiny button nose.

"Hundred," said Armpit.

Ginny **concentrated**. "Hun-dred," she said. "That's a lot of m-money."

"**Tell me about it**," said Armpit.

They were walking around the **block**. Ginny's left hand kept holding on to, then letting go of Armpit. Her right arm was **bent** at the elbow, and **rigid**ly upright, although she wasn't **aware** of it.

"Relax your arm," Armpit **remind**ed her.

Ginny **glanced** at her arm as if it was a **separate being** from herself. It took a moment for her brain to send the proper signals, and then her arm lowered.

She reminded Armpit of a marionette★ who was also her own puppeteer.✱ She had to **figure out** which **string** to pull to make her arms and legs move properly.

She had been born with cerebral palsy.❋ A few neighborhood kids called her spaz,✳ and **retard**, but most treated her with

---

★ **marionette** 마리오네트. 팔, 다리, 머리에 줄을 매달아 움직이는 꼭두각시 인형.
✱ **puppeteer** 인형을 조종하는 사람. 인형극 공연자.
❋ **cerebral palsy** 뇌성 마비.
✳ **spaz** (속어) 바보, 멍청한 녀석.

respect because she was a friend of Armpit's, and because she was willing to answer their questions.

"What's wrong with you?" someone might ask.

If there was a **taunt** in the question she never noticed. "I had **bleed**ing inside my brain wh-when I was born."

And that seemed to satisfy whoever asked the question.

She and her mother had moved into their half of the duplex when Armpit was still at Camp Green Lake. Her mother was ready to move away when she found out that the boy next door was a **violent criminal** who would soon be returning home.

She was now glad she hadn't.

Ginny and Armpit **hit it off** from the beginning. She didn't fear him, and he didn't **pity** her.

Not long after they started their daily walks, Ginny stopped wearing her leg **braces**, **claim**ing they **pinch**ed her. She had a **walker** as well, but only used that if she needed to move quickly, like at school when they went outside for **recess**.

But as much as Armpit helped her, she helped him even more. She gave his life meaning. For the first time in his life, there was someone who **look**ed **up to** him, who cared about him.

Together they were learning to take small steps.

"She s-sings like I talk," said Ginny.

"How do you mean?"

"*H-hands are sh-sh-shaking!*" sang Ginny.

Armpit laughed. "You know that's just part of the song," he said.

"Yes. But I l-like it."

"Me too," said Armpit. "So if you had the money, would you pay fifty-five dollars for a ticket?"

"Yes."

"How about seventy-five?"

"Yes."

"A hundred?"

"No."

He laughed. "They paid seven hundred and fifty dollars in Philadelphia."

"No way!★" said Ginny.

"That's what X-Ray said."

"You c-can't believe everything X-Ray s-says."

She was right about that.

"You sweat a lot." With just one finger **extend**ed, she **delicate**ly touched a large circle of sweat under his arm.

"Yeah, well, it's hot out."

"I don't sweat," said Ginny.

"You will when you get older."

"And I will w-walk and t-talk better."

"Yes, you will," said Armpit. "But sweating's **got nothing to do with** your **disability**. It's just because you haven't reached **puberty** yet."

Ginny **giggle**d.

"What's so funny?"

★ **no way** 기막히거나 놀라서 하는 말. 말도 안돼!

"You s-said puberty."

Armpit laughed too, not at the word, but at her reaction to it.

Ginny was still laughing as they headed up the **crack**ed driveway to their shared house. **Weeds** **poke**d up through the broken cement.

"What are you two laughing at?" asked Ginny's mother, who had come out to the front porch.

"Something," said Ginny.

Armpit winked at her.

Ginny tried to wink back. She closed and opened both her eyes together.

Even though the two families lived inside it, the house was smaller than most of the homes in west Austin where Armpit **plant**ed **shrub**s and **install**ed **irrigation** systems. An **oak** tree in the front yard **shade**d almost the **entire** house.

There were few trees this size in west Austin. That half of the city was mostly built on **solid** white limestone,★ with only a little bit of topsoil✱ above it. Dirt had to be **truck**ed in whenever Raincreek Irrigation and **Landscaping** planted anything.

According to Armpit's father, the cost of **air-conditioning** the homes in west Austin, with their high ceilings and grand **entrances**, was greater than the amount he paid in **rent**.

Armpit's father worked in the daytime as a meter reader★

★ **limestone** 석회석.

✱ **topsoil** 표토. 토양의 가장 윗부분에 위치하는 층.

for the **electric** company. At night he was a **dispatcher** for a **taxicab** company. Armpit's mother worked as a **checker** for H-E-B, a local supermarket chain.

Armpit said good-bye to Ginny and her mother, then went inside. His parents were in the kitchen **chop**ping vegetables.

"Hey, how're things goin'?" his father called.

"They're goin'," Armpit **mutter**ed as he continued down the hall.

"Hold on, I want to talk to you," said his father.

Armpit **sigh**ed. "What about?"

"Just come here."

Armpit stepped into the kitchen. "Look, I been working all afternoon and I'm hot and dirty and **sweaty**. Can't a person just take a shower without **go**ing **through** the third degree?✱"

"No one's **accusing** you of anything," said his mother. "Your dad hardly gets to see you since he started working for Yellow **Cab**.❋"

"Fine, now you can see me," Armpit said.

"I don't **appreciate** your **attitude**," said his father.

"Sorry, I'll change my attitude," Armpit said. "Whatever that means."

"What's wrong with your eyes?" his mother asked him.

"There's nothing wrong with my eyes. I'm tired."

"How you get home?" his father asked.

★ **meter reader** 계량기를 판독하는 사람.

✱ **third degree** 고문. 엄한 심문.

❋ **Yellow Cab** 옐로 캡. 미국의 택시 회사명으로, 영업용 택시를 가리키기도 한다.

"Hernandez."

"I want a sample,★" his father said.

"Why, because he's Mexican? Actually, we were working at the mayor's house. Maybe you think I got **stoned** with the mayor?"

His mother laughed. "I **wouldn't put it past her**."

"The mayor shook my hand," Armpit said. "She said she **admire**d me."

"What'd she mean by that?" asked Armpit's mother.

"You know. Working hard, goin' to school. She'd read about Green Lake."

"And how does she know you were at Green Lake?" his mother asked.

"I guess my boss told her."

"That's supposed to be **confidential**," his mother said. "Those records are supposed to be **seal**ed."

"It's no big secret! Everybody at school knows."

"And that's supposed to make me feel better?"

"I **give up**!" Armpit said.

Most parents would be proud if the mayor said she admired their son!

"I want a sample," his father repeated.

"Why, because I'm tired after working all day?"

"No, because you're being very **defensive**. If you've got nothing to hide . . ."

★ **sample** 마약 등의 성분 테스트를 위한 샘플.

Armpit **march**ed off to the bathroom, where he got a plastic cup out from under the sink.

After he returned from Camp Green Lake, his parents bought a home drug-testing kit.★ They weren't going to **stand by** and let him **ruin** his life, like his brother. He had tried **point**ing **out** that the reason he'd been sent to Green Lake had nothing to do with drugs or alcohol, but that didn't make any difference to them.

"Drugs and alcohol can lead to **violence**," his mother had said.

So could a **bucket** of popcorn.

★ **drug-testing kit** 약물 검사 도구.

4

Armpit showered again in the morning, dried off, then ran a **stick** of **deodorant** three times under each **armpit**. He **splash**ed his face with aftershave lotion.★ He only **shave**d every other day, but he put on aftershave lotion every day.

There was a girl in his speech class who smiled at him a lot **lately**. Her name was Tatiana.

He sprayed Sploosh✱ on his feet. He didn't have a problem with foot **odor**, but when your name was Armpit you had to be extra careful. He sprayed some Sploosh under each armpit for extra **protection**.

One of the guys from Camp Green Lake had sent him a whole case of Sploosh. It was probably meant as a joke, but the guy's father had **invent**ed the **stuff**, so maybe not.

★ **aftershave lotion** 면도 후에 바르는 화장수.

✱ **Sploosh** 전작 『Holes』에 나온 발냄새 탈취제.

The phone was ringing when he stepped out of the bath room. It was X-Ray.

"Hey, partner. You know the six hundred dollars?"

"Yeah, I'm going to stop by the ATM★ after school."

"Good. Only you need to make it six hundred and sixty."

"I thought you were putting up sixty," Armpit **remind**ed him.

"I am," said X-Ray. "I am. The thing is, there's a five-dollar service **charge** on each ticket. So even though the tickets are fifty-five dollars, they cost sixty."

That **made** no **sense** at all.

"Better make it an even seven hundred," said X-Ray. "**Just in case**."

Seven hundred. That would leave him with only a hundred and fifty-seven dollars. A hundred and fifty-seven dollars after three months of working.

"That's not a problem, is it?"

"No. No problem," said Armpit.

"You'll still double your money," X-Ray **assure**d him. "**Guarantee**d. So really, you'll be making more money this way."

Despite all his efforts, he was **sticky** with **sweat** after walking the five **block**s from home to school. At eight-fifty-five in the

★ ATM (= Automatic Teller Machine) 현금 자동 입출기.

✻ **mid-eighties** 화씨 85°F 전후를 말하는 것으로, 섭씨 약 29°C이다.

morning the **temperature** was already in the mid-eighties,★ and the **humid**ity made it seem even hotter.

Tatiana had her back to him when he entered the room. She was talking to her friend Claire. Tatiana had two long **braid**s, which actually connected at the **tip**s, forming a giant V. He'd never seen any other girl wear her hair that way, but everything about Tatiana was a little bit **goofy**. That was what he liked about her. That, and the fact that she smiled at him.

"Hey, Tatiana," he said, trying to sound **casual**, but he was too casual and she didn't hear him. He said it again, a little louder and more **abrupt**ly.

She turned. "What?"

"Uh, nothing. Just wanted to say hi."

"Hi," she said, but without the smile.

Speech class always made him nervous even when there was no speech **due**. Coach Simmons sometimes called on students to speak **extemporaneous**ly. Armpit had a fear of standing at the front of the room, not knowing what to say, sweating, as Tatiana stared at him. He had a hard enough time even when he'd prepared a speech.

Fortunately, there were no extemporaneous speeches this day. Most of the class period was spent discussing the next major **assignment**. Everyone had to bring a **stuffed** animal to school and give a campaign speech★ for it. Then there would be an **election** to see which stuffed animal would be **elect**ed ruler of

---

★ **campaign speech** 선거 연설.

the world.

"I don't even have a stuffed animal," Armpit said aloud as he walked out of the classroom.

There was a laugh, with just a little bit of a **snort** mixed with it. "You are so funny," Tatiana said, touching his arm.

He didn't even know she was there, and hadn't tried to be funny, but he was glad she thought he was.

"I hear you're going out for football next year," she said.

"No, I just wanted Coach Simmons to think that. He gives better grades to football players."

"So you lied to him?" asked Tatiana. "Isn't that kind of **cheat**ing?"

Armpit **shrug**ged.

How could it be cheating? It was unfair that the coach gave better grades to football players, and he was just trying to **even** things **out**. However, by the time he put those thoughts together Tatiana had already walked away.

His other class was **economic**s. Armpit liked Mr. Warren, a **bald**-headed white guy, but he had trouble understanding all the graphs. Somehow by looking at the graphs he was supposed to be able to tell what would happen to the price of a cup of coffee if there was a **drought** in Brazil. It made about as much sense to him as a fifty-five-dollar ticket costing sixty dollars.

Part of his problem was that half the stuff Mr. Warren talked about had nothing to do with the assignments.

"I have here a ten-dollar bill," Mr. Warren said, taking it out of his wallet and holding in the air for all to see. "I'll sell it to the highest **bid**der. Do I hear fifty cents?"

Armpit wasn't quite sure what he meant by that, and he wasn't the only one. Most of the class seemed **confused**, but then Matt Kapok, a kid in the front **row**, **offer**ed fifty cents.

"Going once, going twice—★"

"Wait a second," said the girl who sat next to Armpit. "You mean you're going to sell your ten-dollar bill to Matt for fifty cents?"

"Yep," said Mr. Warren. "Unless I get a better offer."

"Sure, I'll give you sixty cents for it," said the girl.

Someone else offered seventy-five cents, then a dollar, and before too long it was up to nine dollars and ninety-nine cents. And then someone bid ten dollars, **trading** his ten-dollar bill for Mr. Warren's.

There was a lesson in all that, but Armpit wasn't quite sure exactly what it was.

"One year I actually sold it for ten dollars and ten cents," Mr. Warren told the class.

Eighteen hundred miles away, Kaira DeLeon was getting her own lesson in economics.

"I just want to know how much money I made so far," she said.

"It's not that simple, dear," said her mother.

★ **going once, going twice** 더 입찰 하실 분 없습니까, 없습니까. 경매에서 낙찰하기 전에 하는 말.

"I'm not asking *you*," said Kaira.

Her mother had on an aqua★ and indigo✱ silk jacket, with a small **sapphire pin**ned to the **lapel**. Kaira hadn't seen either the jacket or the pin before, but that wasn't surprising. Her mother seemed to show up with a new **outfit** daily.

"I can't give you exact **figures**," said Jerome Paisley, Kaira's **agent** and business manager.

He had just returned from the hotel's health club, and was still wearing his running shorts and a V-neck undershirt. A gold chain **hung** around his thick neck.

He had a large **forehead** and a **puffy** face, which was no doubt the result of taking steroids.❋ At one time he'd been a pro baseball player, although, except for eighteen days, he'd never made it out of the minor leagues.✳ His career was **ruin**ed after he was hit in the face by a **pitch**.

Kaira always wondered how someone could get hit in the face by a pitch. *You have to see it coming, don't you?*

"Have I made a million dollars yet?" she asked.

"There are a lot of **expenses**. Do you even know how many people are on this tour?"

She was too **embarrass**ed to say she didn't, so she remained silent.

"Forty-two," said Jerome Paisley. "Everyone gets **salaries**,

---

★ **aqua** 청록색.
✱ **indigo** 남색.
❋ **steroids** 스테로이드. 운동 선수들이 복용하는 지방 융해성 화학물.
✳ **minor league** 마이너리그. 프로 야구 하위 팀들의 리그이다.

per diems, travel expenses. And then there are **additional** costs **associated** with each **venue**."

"What's my salary?"

"You don't get a salary. You get what's left over after everyone else is paid."

"You're doing very well, sweetie," said her mother.

"How much does the Doofus get paid?" Kaira asked.

"I've asked you not to call him that," said her mother.

"I just want to know. How much do you have to pay a **babysitter**?"

"Fred gets fourteen hundred a week, plus expenses," said her business manger, her mother's husband.

Kaira laughed. "And what about your new jacket?" she asked her mother. "Who paid for that?"

"Your money all goes into a trust **account**,★" said her mother's husband. "Nobody can touch it, not even your mother. You'll **get it** when you turn eighteen."

"Yeah, well, a lot is going to happen when I turn eighteen," Kaira said.

If Jerome Paisley heard the **threat**, he chose not to **acknowledge** it. "It doesn't really matter even if you don't make a dime✻ on this tour," he told her. "Right now, it's all about **exposure**. Getting your name out there. Getting your songs on the radio. You'll make more money in CD sales than you'll ever

★ **trust account** 신탁계정. 재산을 대신 맡아 운용해 주는 계좌를 말한다.
✻ **dime** 다임. 10센트 동전.

make on the tour."

"Maybe we should charge more for the tickets," Kaira suggested.

"Oh, you think so?"

She didn't like his **patronizing** tone.

"In Philadelphia, tickets went for seven hundred and fifty dollars," she said, trying to show that she knew a thing or two.

"Where'd you hear that?"

"I don't know," Kaira said, suddenly feeling **defensive**. "On the radio, I think."

He **smirk**ed at her. "I **plant**ed that story," he **boast**ed. "You didn't even **sell out** in Philly." He pointed to his big, fat head and said, "El Genius at work."

Kaira felt foolish.

"The most important thing in this business isn't **talent**," he told her. "It's all about **hype**. Hype and **buzz**."

"Well, it still makes me mad that ticket **scalper**s make the money instead of me."

"You let me worry about the business end of things. You just keep singing and shaking that sexy little body."

"Listen to what Jerome tells you," said Kaira's mother. She gave her husband a kiss on his puffy cheek. "He's made you what you are."

5

X-Ray picked Armpit up at four o'clock in the morning, and they drove to the Lonestar **Arena**. "Anything in the first row is pure gold," he said. "Pure gold. The second row too. Anything in the first two rows."

Armpit brought his economics book along. He knew he'd probably miss speech, but there was a test in econ★ and he couldn't **afford** to miss that.

When they **pull**ed **into** the parking lot, they saw that a line had already formed at the ticket window. Tickets wouldn't go on sale until eight o'clock.

"Man, I told you we should have spent the night here," X-Ray said.

"You never said that."

"Well, I thought it."

★ econ 'economics(경제학)'의 줄임말.

They got in line. There were already twenty-nine people ahead of them in line. X-Ray counted it twice.

Armpit lay on his back in the **gravel** parking lot with his eyes closed. His economics book was his **pillow**. He planned to study when there was enough light. A piece of gravel dug into his back, but the more he tried to **smooth** it out the worse it got, so he did his best to **ignore** it.

Somebody in line had brought a boom box,★ and *The Fountain of Youth*, Kaira DeLeon's CD, was playing. Armpit was lying there, his eyes closed, only half listening, when he suddenly heard her sing:

These shoes, these jewels, this dress,
A perfect picture of success.
Oh, you would never guess, Armpit,
*A **damsel in distress**.*✵

At least, that was what it sounded like.

Save me, Armpit!
A damsel in distress.

He sat up. "Did you hear that?"

"Hear what?" asked X-Ray.

★ **boom box** 대형 휴대용 카세트 라디오.
✵ **damsel in distress** 비탄에 빠진 소녀. 책 제목으로 사용되기도 하는 관용구이다.

"Never mind."

If he told him, X-Ray would never let him **live** it **down**. Why would she sing "Armpit"? It was impossible. There was no possible way. He must have fallen asleep for a second and dreamed it.

In line behind them were five men who seemed especially dirty and **ragged**. Armpit might have guessed they were **street people**, except for the fact that they were waiting in line to buy sixty-dollar tickets. From the way they smelled, he thought maybe they worked for the **sanitation department** and had come here after work.

"I'm thinking third row," X-Ray said. "Third or fourth. As long as we're somewhere in the first five rows we're golden."

Armpit looked at the people in line ahead of him. Nearly all were white, even though Kaira DeLeon was African American. Several wore shirts and ties.

"I don't know," he said. "If everybody buys six tickets—"

"Not everyone's going to buy six tickets," X-Ray **interrupted**. "Besides, you really don't want to be too close. It's better to be a few rows back. The best seats are between row three and row seven. Those are the ones that will bring in the big money."

Shortly after sunrise, Armpit opened his book and tried to understand the difference between fixed costs★ and **variable** costs.✳ Graphs **illustrated** how these changed as more **goods**

★ **fixed cost** [경제학] 고정 비용.
✳ **variable cost** [경제학] 변동 비용.

were produced. The line **represent**ing fixed costs was flat, and the one representing variable costs **angle**d upward.

It **might as well** have been written in Chinese.

"Look at all the people behind us!" X-Ray **point**ed **out**. "They'd pay a hundred dollars just to have our place in line."

"I'll take it," said Armpit.

X-Ray laughed. "We're going to make a lot more than that, my friend. A lot more."

After a while a guy wearing a Lonestar Arena T-shirt came out and tried to **adjust** the line so that instead of **stick**ing straight **out** from the ticket window, it went **parallel** to the building. This caused a lot of **grumbling** from the **grubby** guys sitting behind Armpit.

"What difference does it make?"

"I was just gettin' comfortable."

"Just because you got the T-shirt doesn't make you God!"

But they got up and moved along with everyone else.

The mystery of who they were was solved shortly after seven-thirty, when the guys who were paying them showed up. One was a fast-talking, **skinny** white guy. With him was a big **dude** wearing a cowboy hat and boots.

"Now listen up, 'cause I'm not going to repeat myself," said the skinny guy. He wore a pearl earring and had a face that needed to make a choice—either **shave** or grow a **beard**. "When you get to the ticket window, Moses here will give you an **envelope** containing three hundred and thirty dollars. You don't have to count it. You just hand it to the ticket **agent** and ask for six tickets. You then give the tickets to Moses, and he will pay you twenty-five dollars."

"Twenty-five dollars!" **complain**ed one of the guys. "We've been sitting here for five hours! I could make more than that sitting on the corner of Mopac and Spicewood."

"You want to go, go," said the skinny guy. The big guy in the cowboy hat—Moses, **apparent**ly—had a **thermos** of coffee and a bag of breakfast tacos,★ which he handed out. He tried to give Armpit a taco.

"I'm not one of them," Armpit said, **somewhat offend**ed.

"We're not part of your **crew**," said X-Ray.

"Oh yeah?" said the skinny one. "Just a Kaira DeLeon fan, are you?"

"We're **independent**," said X-Ray.

"Well, we got a couple of extra tacos if you want 'em."

Armpit and X-Ray looked at each other, then happily took the tacos.

Moses filled a Styrofoam✱ cup of coffee for X-Ray. Armpit didn't drink coffee.

"I'm Felix," said the skinny guy. "This is my man Moses."

"X-Ray," said X-Ray. "And that's my man Armpit."

"Armpit, huh?"

"A **scorpion**—"

★ **taco** 타코. 멕시코의 대표적인 음식으로 옥수수를 으깨어 얇게 원형으로 구워서 만든 토르티야를 U자형으로 만들어 튀긴 후 그 속에다 고기, 콩, 양상추, 치즈 등을 넣고 칠리 소스를 뿌려 먹는 음식이다.

✱ **Styrofoam** [상표명] 스티로폼.

"Tell you what," said Felix. "After you get your tickets, come talk to me."

"We're going to have to leave straight away," said Armpit. "I got an economics test."

"Listen to me, Armpit," said Felix. "I bring you a breakfast taco, the least you can do is talk to me. If you're studying econ, then you should know. There's no such thing as a free lunch.★"

The ticket windows didn't open until ten after eight, and the line moved **excruciating**ly slowly.

"C'mon, c'mon. How long does it take to buy a ticket?" X-Ray **yell**ed at the people in front of him.

There were two ticket windows. X-Ray went first, and when Armpit reached the one next to him, he could hear X-Ray **arguing** with the ticket agent. "Are you sure this is the best you got? Well, can you check?"

Armpit paid for his tickets. They were all in row M. He counted in his head. The thirteenth row. On the back of each ticket, printed in **bold** letters, were the words *This ticket may not be resold.*

"M's good," said X-Ray. "It's the first half of the alphabet. That's all that matters. Just look at all those fools still waiting in line!" He laughed. "They'll be lucky if they're in the same zip

★ **There's no such thing as a free lunch** [속담] 세상에 공짜 점심은 없다.

code."

Armpit pointed out what was written on the back of each ticket, but X-Ray wasn't concerned. "They can write anything they want. It doesn't mean **squat**. This is America. Everything's for sale."

They watched as Moses paid the last member of his crew.

"Those guys are so cool," X-Ray said. "That could be us in a few years."

Felix headed toward them. "So, X-Ray, you get good seats?"

"Row M!"

"M's good," said Felix. "First half of the alphabet."

"That's what I was tellin' Armpit."

"The first few rows are **reserve**d for friends and radio **station**s. It's a **rip-off**, but what can you do?"

"What can you do?" X-Ray agreed.

"Tell you what. I'll give you seventy **buck**s for each ticket. That's fifteen more than face **value**. Times twelve, you'll make a hundred and eighty dollars. Ninety bucks each."

"They cost sixty, not fifty-five," said Armpit.

"Yeah I know," said Felix. "There's a five-dollar service **charge**. What a rip-off. But the thing is, you try to sell the tickets, and all the customer's gonna see is the face value."

"We're not interested," said X-Ray.

"All right, I'll pay the damn★ service charge. Seventy-five a ticket."

★ **damn** [속어] 제기랄, 빌어먹을, 젠장.

"We can do a lot better," said X-Ray.

"Maybe," Felix agreed. "Maybe you can. I'm not saying you can't. But you never know. A bird in the hand.★ Ninety dollars, Armpit, for just a morning's work. Hard to **beat** that."

"We're not interested," said X-Ray.

"Armpit looks interested. How about it, Armpit?"

It did sound pretty good to him. Ninety dollars was more than he made in two days of digging.

"They sold for seven hundred and fifty in Philly," said X-Ray.

"Austin ain't Philly," said Felix. "And row M ain't exactly the front row."

"We were ahead of your guys in line," said X-Ray. "Whatever we got has to be better than anything you got."

"Look, I'm not saying you couldn't make more than seventy-five dollars a ticket. I wouldn't be talkin' to you if I didn't think so. But there's **risk**, too. Right now, things are looking pretty good. Big **demand**. Short **supply**. The price can only go up. But there was a big demand when Dylan✳ played here a few years back. So you know what they did? They added a second show. You're the economist, Armpit. You know what happens when supply goes up?"

"The price goes down?"

"Like an elevator with a **busted** **cable**. I was lucky to **unload**

★ **A bird in the hand (is worth two in the bush)** [속담] 손 안에 든 새 한 마리가 숲 속에 있는 두 마리보다 낫다.

✳ **Bob Dylan** 밥 딜런. 미국의 가수.

my **inventory**. Or what do you think would happen if we learn that sweet little Miss Kaira is **pregnant**? Or say she burns the American flag in some kind of **political protest**? I can tell you what would happen. You wouldn't be able to give your tickets away."

"Yeah, well, if it's so risky, then why do you want the tickets so badly?" asked X-Ray.

"This is my business. If I lose money on Kaira DeLeon, I'll make it up next week on someone else. You're going to have to put an **ad** in the paper. That costs money. Me, I already got a **run**ning ad. It costs me the same no matter how many tickets I'm selling."

"A fixed cost," Armpit said as it all suddenly **made sense** to him.

"And I got connections, too," Felix went on. "Every hotel **concierge** knows who to call if some guest wants tickets. All I'm sayin' is, it's not as easy as you think for a couple of independents. I'm offering you a hundred and eighty dollars, pure **profit**, and no worries."

"We ain't worried," said X-Ray.

"Armpit looks worried."

"I'm cool," said Armpit. Felix smiled. "Then why are you sweating so much?"

"Don't you worry. We're going to make a lot more than ninety bucks **apiece**," X-Ray assured him as they drove out of the parking lot. "A lot more. Felix wouldn'ta wanted to buy them if he didn't think so. This is a great day! We're on our way, partner! We are on our way!"

By the time they reached the high school, Armpit was already five minutes late for his test. As he was getting out of the car, X-Ray said, "By the way. I'm going to need thirty bucks to put an ad in the paper."

6

He was walking home from school an hour later when a man coming the other way crossed to the other side of the street. It was no **big deal**, and maybe the guy really needed to cross the street, but that kind of thing happened a lot to Armpit. White people did it more, but African Americans did it too. He usually **pretend**ed not to notice, but sometimes he'd give the guy a **menacing glare** as if to say, "Yeah, you better stay out of my way!"

This time he just **ignore**d it. He was in too good a **mood** to glare.

He'd gotten a ninety on his **economic**s test, thanks to Felix. He'd learned more in the parking lot of the Lonestar Arena than he had learned all year in class.

"It all just **click**ed," he told Ginny as they took their daily walk. "Even the graphs! The questions were all about people buying and selling everything from **gasoline** to hula hoops,★ but in my own mind, I put it **in terms of** tickets."

"Hula hoops," Ginny said with a laugh. "That's funny!"

After their walk, he asked her if he could borrow a **stuffed** animal for his ruler-of-the-world speech.

Ginny was amazed. Hula hoops, stuffed animals, ruler of the world—high school sounded a lot more fun than the fourth grade.

She led him into her room, where she had more than thirty stuffed animals.

"Just give me one you don't like too much," Armpit said.

"I love all of them," Ginny said, but not in a **selfish** way. She **definite**ly **consider**ed it an **honor** for one of her lovies✳ to get to go to high school with Theodore, and she carefully considered who was most **deserving**.

"How about that one," Armpit said, indicating a brown owl with huge eyes.

"That's Hoo-**Hooter**,❋" said Ginny. "He can't see."

"He can't?"

"He's **blind**. But he can h-hear really g-good and so he never b-**bump**s into trees."

"How can he hear trees?" Armpit asked.

"The leaves **rustle** in the wind," said Ginny.

Ginny must have said that same sentence many times before because she didn't **stutter** over any of the words.

★ **hula hoop** 훌라후프.

✳ **lovie** 애정을 담아 표현하는 말. 사랑스러운 친구들.

❋ **hooter** hoot은 '부엉부엉'을 말하는데, 여기에서 부엉이의 이름을 딴 것이다.

"This is Daisy," she said, handing Armpit a basset hound,★ with long, **floppy** ears.

"How ya doin', Daisy?" said Armpit.

"She c-can't hear you," said Ginny. "She's **deaf**. But she has a **keen** sense of smell."

Armpit smiled. He liked it that she used the word "keen."

The next one she showed him was Roscoe, a **fuzzy** bear with **twist**y arms and legs. Roscoe was **paralyze**d due to a "**horrible** accident."

Ginny sat on the **edge** of the bed with her legs **bow**ed out and her toes pointed downward. As a baby she couldn't learn to walk because she was always on **tiptoe**. She had to wear a special **brace** just to straighten out her feet.

Armpit looked over the three animals. Hooter was out. Everyone would just laugh at the name.

"Oh, I know!" Ginny suddenly **exclaim**ed as she brought both hands to her face. "You need Coo!✳"

Coo was a sort of **bunny** creature lying next to Ginny's bed. It had arms and legs like a person but had bunny ears.

"I've had Coo my whole life," Ginny said.

"I better just take Roscoe," said Armpit.

Ginny **frown**ed.

"I think Coo's great," Armpit **assure**d her. "I just don't want to take your favorite. It's just a stupid speech. What if

★ **basset hound** [동물] 바셋 하운드. 다리가 짧은 사냥개이다.
✳ **Coo** '정답게 소곤거리다', '구구 울다'라는 뜻의 이름이다.

something happens?"

"Coo isn't scared," said Ginny. "He is always strong and brave. H-he will be the b-best ruler of the w-w-world!"

"Well, I wouldn't **count on** Coo winning," Armpit cautioned. "I get real nervous when I have to give a speech."

"Coo will help you," said Ginny.

Armpit held Coo in one hand. It was soft and **spongy**, the kind of toy given to babies because it was easily held on to by tiny fingers. "So is there something wro—" He caught himself. "Does Coo have a **disability**?" he asked.

"Leukemia,★" Ginny **whisper**ed. "But we don't talk about it."

★ **leukemia** 백혈병.

7

Friday, with the concert just eight days away, Armpit went to the Stop & Shop after school to buy a newspaper. He had paid thirty dollars for the **ad**; he **might as well** pay another fifty cents to see it.

He dropped two quarters★ into the newspaper **vending machine** and pulled up on the handle, but it wouldn't open. He pressed the coin return and got back nothing. He pulled harder on the handle. He **slam**med his hand against the coin return.✵

He was already mad that X-Ray had waited two days to buy the ad because he only wanted to pay for one week, and now the machine had eaten his money. He shook it so hard he might have broken it, but then a voice in his head **remind**ed him that it wasn't **worth** going to jail for fifty cents.

★ **quarter** 쿼터. 미국 · 캐나다의 25센트 동전. 4분의 1달러.

✵ **coin return** 동전(coin) 반환(return)구.

Instead, he went into the store and told the **clerk** what had happened.

"You have to wait for the coins to drop," the guy told him, and wouldn't give him his money back.

Armpit asked him for change for a dollar.

"No change."

So he bought a bag of chips for a dollar and nineteen cents, then used part of the change to buy another paper.

This time he listened for each quarter to drop before pulling on the handle. When the door opened, he took three copies of the *Austin American Statesman*, just to **get even**, and left two of them on top of the machine.

Back home, he spread the **classified** ads out across the kitchen table. He'd told X-Ray not to ask for too much, since they only had a week. There were a number of ads for Kaira DeLeon tickets. The prices **ranged** from seventy-five to a hundred and ten dollars. Then he came to the one with X-Ray's phone number.

Kaira DeLeon Tkts. $135

Close to the front. 555–3470

X-Ray answered on the second ring.

"Are you **insane**?" Armpit shouted.

"Yes, but it hasn't stopped me before!"

"Did you see all the other ads in the paper?"

"Yeah, so?"

"So they're all at least twenty-five dollars cheaper."

"And your point is?"

"I told you to keep the price low."

"It is low. They sold for seven hundred and fifty in Philly."

"We're not going to be able to sell any tickets."

"You're thinking east Austin," said X-Ray. "You got to think west Austin."

"*What?*"

"See, you and me, we'd buy the cheapest tickets. But that's not how they think in west Austin. They don't worry about money over there. They just want the best. And the ones that cost the most got to be the best, right?"

Armpit had **install**ed enough **sprinkler** systems in west Austin to know that people worried about money over there just as much as they did east of I-35.★ Their homes might have been worth half a million dollars, but they still expected Armpit's boss to **reimburse** them five **buck**s if Armpit **accidental**ly stepped on a daffodil.✻

"Okay," Armpit said. "Even if somebody wanted to pay a little more to be up front," he said, "**row** M is *not* the front!"

"The ad doesn't say it's in the front. It says *close to* the front."

"It's not close to the front. Row F is close to the front. G maybe."

★ **I-35** Interstate 35번.
✻ **daffodil** [식물] 수선화.

"So then they're *close to* close to the front," said X-Ray.

"Just call the paper and tell them to lower the price," said Armpit.

"You need to relax. I promised you I'd double your money, didn't I? Didn't I?"

Double or nothing, thought Armpit.

"Besides, it'll cost another ten bucks to change the ad."

He didn't sleep that night, or the next night, or the night after that. X-Ray didn't sell a single ticket over the weekend.

He wondered how he had ever let X-Ray talk him into this. Why didn't they sell the tickets to Felix when they had the chance? Now he was out another thirty dollars for the ad in the paper, and it would cost ten more to change it.

But at three o'clock Monday morning, he decided that was what they would have to do. Just change the ad. Seventy-five dollars. They'd still make a small **profit**. Maybe if they had gotten seats in the first or second row they could have **held out for** more money, but now they just needed to **get rid of** the tickets before it was too late.

At four o'clock in the morning he decided on seventy dollars a ticket.

"That's five dollars less than Felix **offer**ed!" X-Ray said when Armpit called him before going to school.

"Well, we should have sold them to Felix when we had the chance," Armpit said. "But we didn't, and now I just want to get the things sold."

"For seventy dollars?"

"We'll still come out ahead, even after the cost of the ad."

"So you don't want to sell them for a hundred and thirty-five?"

"That's what I said. Look, it's my money **on the line**."

"That's a problem," said X-Ray.

"I'll pay the ten dollars!"

"It's not that," said X-Ray. "It's just . . ."

"Now what?"

X-Ray **heave**d a heavy **sigh**. "Well, a guy just called and he wants to buy two tickets at a hundred and thirty-five. He's meeting me after he **gets off** work. I guess I'll just call him back and tell him they only cost seventy." He laughed. "I mean, if that's what you want me to do." He laughed again.

Armpit managed a smile.

Later at work he had to remove a red **tip** photinia★ from someone's yard, and its root was **enormous**. He first cut off the **bush** at the base, then started on the root, but no matter how deep he dug, he never could seem to get to the bottom of it. It was like an **octopus** with thick, long **tentacle**s that hugged the ground.

He went at it with an **axe**, **hack**ing off many of its **offshoot**s, but **to no avail**. Finally he wrapped a chain around it and

★ **photinia** [식물] 홍가시나무.

attached the other end to the back of a **pickup truck**.

He climbed into the **cab**, put it into four-wheel drive,★ and **shift**ed into first gear.✳ There was a moment of **uncertainty**, and he worried he might **destroy** the engine, but then the root **pop**ped **out** of the ground.

He lifted it into the back of the pickup along with the top half of the bush. He was hot, tired, **sore**, and covered with dirt and **sweat**.

But he felt good. He had a feeling of **satisfaction** that he could never explain to X-Ray. It was good clean work. **Scalp**ing tickets felt dirty in **comparison**.

★ four-wheel drive 사륜 구동.

✳ first gear 1단 기어.

8

He and Ginny waited out front for X-Ray to bring the money from the ticket sales.

"Two hun-hundred and seventy dollars," said Ginny. "If you s-sell ten more . . ." She did the math aloud. "Ten times one hundred and thirty-five is one thousand three hundred and fifty!" Her eyes **widen**ed. "You're rich!"

Armpit laughed. "Well, I'll have to **split** the profits with X-Ray. When we sell all the tickets I'll make a profit of four hundred and thirty-five dollars." He had done the math too. "You know, you didn't **stutter** at all when you were adding," he **point**ed **out**.

"I only stutter when I t-t-t-talk."

"You were talking."

"That was math. I'm g-good with numbers. Not w-w-words."

"Well, you're pretty smart," he said.

"And you're pretty rich."

"And you're pretty cute."

"And you're pretty pretty."

She laughed at her own joke.

"What's so funny?"

"I s-said you were pretty."

"So?"

"G-girls are pretty. Boys are handsome. That m-means you're a girl!"

"And you're pretty silly," said Armpit.

He noticed a woman watching them from the parking lot of the Stop & Shop. He wondered if she was **suspicious** because he was with a little white girl. Did she think they were on drugs? Maybe she was memorizing his face, in case it **turn**ed **out** the girl had been **abduct**ed.

He stared back at the woman, who then quickly got into her car and drove away.

Or maybe she just enjoyed seeing two people smiling and laughing.

The X-Mobile passed her coming in the other direction.

"There's X-Ray," said Ginny.

Not **bother**ing with a U-turn, X-Ray parked facing the wrong way. He slid over to the **passenger** side, climbed out, then walked around the car.

"Hey, Ginny. You taking good care of Armpit?"

"Yes."

"So, did you sell the tickets?" Armpit asked.

X-Ray smiled. "See, Ginny, that's what I like about Armpit. Straight to the point. No **bull**—" He stopped himself. "No bull."

"He d-doesn't like to be called Armpit."

"I mean it with great **respect** and **affection**," X-Ray said, his hand on his heart.

"Did you sell the tickets?" Armpit asked again.

"Say, Ginny, did I ever tell you what happened to my car?" X-Ray asked, pointing to the big **gash** in the driver-side door.

"No."

"I'm driving along Mopac, and this **dinosaur** leaps out and takes a big bite out of my door! Scared me half to death!"

Ginny laughed.

"Look, do you see the teeth marks?"

Ginny pushed back her glasses on her nose. "Yes."

"I think it was a T. rex!★ Can you believe it?"

"No."

X Ray laughed.

"So you didn't sell the tickets, did you?" said Armpit.

"Okay, here's the deal," said X-Ray. I was supposed to meet the **dude** in the parking lot of the H-E-B at five-fifteen. Hey, Ginny, you know what H-E-B **stands for**?"

"No."

"Howard E. Butt. Seriously. That was the man's name. That's why they just call it H-E-B. Would you want to buy

---

★ T. rex 공룡 티라노사우루스.

your **groceries** at a place called Butt's?"

Ginny **cracked up**.

Armpit **glared** at X-Ray.

"Okay, so anyway," X-Ray continued, "I get there at five o'clock, fifteen minutes early. So then I wait. The guy said he'd be driving a white Suburban.★ Five-fifteen: no white Suburban. Five-twenty-five. Five-thirty. It's like a hundred and fifty degrees✴ in the parking lot, but still I wait 'cause I don't want to **let** my buddy Armpit **down**. Finally, at five-thirty-five, I hear this guy screaming out, 'X-Ray! X-Ray!' like some kind of **maniac**. So I give a couple a toot-toots❋ and then this **obese** vehicle **pulls up** beside me and two ol'✶ rednecks✴ get out. 'Are you X-Ray?'

"'No, I'm just some dude who happens to have X-Ray on his **license** plate'—but I don't say that. I say, 'Yeah, that's me,' and I'm just about to hand over the tickets when he asks, now get this, Ginny, he asks who he should make the **check** out to.

"I tell him he can make the check out to the tooth fairy★ for all I care. He goes into this whole **riff** about losing his ATM card, which was why he was late, but I don't want to hear it."

"So you didn't sell the tickets?" asked Armpit.

★ **Suburban** 쉐보레(Chevrolet)사에서 나오는 차.

✴ **a hundred and fifty degrees** 화씨 150°F는 섭씨 약 65°C이다.

❋ **toot** 빵, 삑. 자동차 경적 또는 호루라기 소리.

✶ **ol'** old.

✴ **redneck** 미국 남부 농촌의 백인 노동자.

★ **tooth fairy** 이의 요정. 밤에 어린 아이의 침대 머리맡에 빠진 이를 놓아두면 이것을 가져가고 그 대신에 동전을 놓아둔다는 상상 속의 존재이다.

"They still want 'em," said X-Ray. "They're going to meet me back at the H-E-B at ten tonight. They say they'll have the cash this time. Only, you better come with."

"I can't. I got econ homework, a speech to write—man, I thought you were supposed to do all the work. I just put up the money."

"They were two big white guys. And there won't be too many people around at ten o'clock. I just think it's a good idea to have some **backup**."

Armpit didn't like where this was heading.

"Don't worry. One look at you and there won't be any trouble."

For better or for worse, Armpit knew that was probably true.

He worked on his Coo speech until it was time to go, first making an **outline**, then putting his key points on three-by-five cards.★ His speech was mostly about Ginny and how important Coo was to her. He **came up with** a sentence he really liked: *Coo gives her **comfort**, courage, and **confidence**.*

He realized he might be taking the **assignment** a little too seriously. The people who had given their speeches earlier today had treated the **election** as if it was a big joke, which of course it was. One girl had **urged** everyone to **vote** for

★ **three-by-five cards** 세로 3인치, 가로 5인치로 된 종이 카드. 연설이나 발표 내용의 요점 사항들을 적어 두는 데 사용되고, 손바닥 크기만하다 하여 palm cards라고도 불린다.

Milford the Monkey because if he became ruler of the world, he would **plant** a million banana trees, and that would stop the **destruction** of the **rain forest**s and help **prevent global warming**. Another kid urged everyone to vote for Wilbur the Pig because he would **bring about** world peace, and if he didn't, then at least everyone would get a ham sandwich.

But Armpit knew he wasn't good at making jokes, and if he didn't write his speech down, he would just stand there, sweating and **babbling** nervously. Besides, he really wanted Coo to win, **for** Ginny's **sake**.

X-Ray showed up a little before ten.

"Where **are** you **off** to?" Armpit's mother demanded.

"We just got to do something," Armpit said as he hurried outside, knowing he'd have to **submit** a sample when he returned.

It was the same H-E-B where his mother worked, although it had been a few years since she'd had to work the night **shift**. There were only a few cars in the parking lot, and no white Suburban.

"Man, I'm getting sick of getting **jerk**ed **around** by those **joker**s!" X-Ray **complain**ed.

"Just give 'em a couple of minutes," said Armpit. "He did say he lost his ATM card. Maybe he's having trouble getting the cash together."

"A couple a minutes," X-Ray agreed. "And then we're out of here. It's **disrespect**. What, they think we got nothing better to do than wait around for them? Disrespect."

Armpit was feeling **claustrophobic** in the car and stepped out to **stretch**.

"Good idea," said X-Ray. "Let 'em get a good look at you."

He looked up and down the **aisles**. "Maybe they're waiting at the other end of the parking lot," he suggested.

"I'm in the exact **spot** where I was earlier. The exact spot."

At a quarter after there was still no sign of them. "That's it," X-Ray **announced**. "We're leaving."

"Just wait a few more—" Armpit started, but X-Ray had already started the engine.

Armpit climbed back in, and they had only just started moving when a large white SUV★ **pulled into** the lot.

"Is that them?" Armpit asked.

X-Ray continued to drive away.

"Wait! It's a white Suburban."

"Too late!" X-Ray said as they **bounced** over a speed **bump**.

The **horn** sounded on the Suburban.

X-Ray **yell**ed an **obscenity** out his window, then **lurch**ed out of the parking lot and into **traffic**.

"Are you **nuts**?" Armpit yelled. "That's two hundred and seventy dollars!"

"Our respect is worth a lot more than that," said X-Ray. "Who do they think they are?"

"If you don't sell the tickets, I'm going to kill you," Armpit

★ SUV (= Sport Utility Vehicle) 스포츠형의 다목적 자동차.

warned him.

X-Ray laughed. “Always the joker.”

9

Armpit felt pretty silly carrying Coo to school on Tuesday, and wished he had taken his backpack. He was still mad at X-Ray, but he was even madder at himself. The concert was four days away and no tickets had been sold. Six hundred and ninety dollars down the toilet.

"Hey, Armpit, want a ride?"

He **glance**d over to see a yellow Mustang★ slowly moving along beside him.

"Where you going, Armpit?"

There were five people in the car, three guys and two girls, and although he only **recognize**d the two guys in the front seat, he knew he didn't want anything to do with any of them. The driver was named Donnell, and the guy beside him was

★ Mustang 포드(Ford)사에서 나온 차.

Cole. Both were three or four years older than he was, and he was sort of surprised they knew his name. It was not good news.

"Come on, **hop in**," said Cole. "We'll take you where you want to go."

The **trick** was to say no without **offend**ing anyone, especially Cole, who was known to be a little bit crazy.

"It doesn't look like you got much room," Armpit said.

He wondered what they were doing out so early in the morning, then realized they must have been up all night. They were probably **high**.

"Always room for a brother. Sharese can sit on your **lap**."

"That's okay," said Armpit as he continued to walk. "I'm fine walking." He continued to walk and the car rolled slowly **alongside** him.

"What's the matter? You don't like Sharese?"

"Hi, Armpit," called a girl in the backseat.

"I just like to walk, that's all."

The car pulled ahead of him, and for a second he thought they were **through with** him, but then it **swerved** sharply into a driveway, **block**ing his path. The passenger door★ opened.

"You know, when a brother **offer**s you a ride," said Cole, "the right thing to do is accept."

"I didn't mean any **disrespect**," Armpit said.

At least they all remained inside the car. He tried to act

★ **passenger door** 조수석 문.

casual.

"What's with the **bunny**?" asked Sharese.

Armpit **tighten**ed his **grip** on Coo. "Something for school."

"School! It's summer!" shouted one of the guys from the back.

"It's so cute," Sharese said. "Can I have it?"

"It's for a school project."

"I want it," said Sharese.

Armpit tightened his grip on Coo. "It belongs to my neighbor." He'd fight all of them if he had to, before **giving** Coo **up**.

"That little white **retard**!" said Cole. "I seen you hangin' with her. Man, what's her problem?" He laughed.

Cole wasn't expecting an answer, but Armpit copied Ginny's **tactic** and gave him one.

"There was some **bleed**ing inside her brain when she was born."

"Oh," Cole said. "Too bad."

Armpit slowly walked around the Mustang.

"What are you going to school for?" Cole shouted at him. "Come work with us, and you'll make all the money you'll ever need."

"Thanks, but it's just something I got to do."

He kept walking.

He heard the car door shut behind him but didn't turn around. A moment later he saw the car driving past him. Someone shouted "Fool!" out the window.

Fifteen minutes later he stood in front of the class, all eyes on him, including Tatiana's.

"This is Coo," he began.

Everybody laughed.

"Coo has leukemia."

Some even laughed at that, too.

It wasn't that they were **cruel**. All the other speeches had been **humorous** and they expected more of the same. The sight of Armpit, the biggest and toughest kid in class, holding the little baby toy just added to the comedy, and it took a while for what he was saying to **sink in**.

He could feel his **sweat dripping** down his side and hoped it didn't show on his shirt.

"Coo belongs to my neighbor, Ginny. She has cerebral palsy."

"You just said she had leukemia," said Claire, Tatiana's friend.

"Coo has leukemia. Ginny has cerebral palsy. That's why Coo should be **elect**ed ruler of the world. Because Coo gives her **comfort**, courage, and **confidence**."

That was supposed to be his closing sentence. He didn't mean to say it so soon. He **fumble**d with his notecards, but he'd already gotten off wrong, so he just **wing**ed **it**.

"All her life, Ginny has had trouble walking and talking. Some kids at her school call her 'tard, you know, short for retard, but she's not retarded. She's really smart. It's just that her brain has difficulty **process**ing information. It's like she has to **decode** everything first. That's why she stutters when she talks. She knows what she wants to say, but it's like her brain has trouble sending the signal to her mouth. And then if people **pressure** her, it just gets worse and worse, and she sometimes has these **spastic seizures**."

"And you want her to be ruler of the world?" somebody asked. Several people laughed.

"No, you should **vote** for Coo, Ginny's favorite **stuffed** animal. See, since I don't own any stuffed animals, Ginny gave me Coo. I told her I didn't want her favorite, you know, 'cause it's just for a stupid **assignment**."

The class **erupt**ed in laughter and Armpit realized that he probably shouldn't have called it a stupid assignment in front of Coach Simmons. He **pressed on**. "But Ginny said I had to take Coo. She said none of her others were as strong or as brave as Coo. Well, even though Ginny is only ten years old and has cerebral palsy and **weigh**s less than sixty pounds,★ she's the strongest and bravest person I know. So if Coo could do that for Ginny, imagine what Coo could do for the world. So vote for Coo. Thanks."

He made his way back to his seat without looking at anyone. He had no idea if anything he'd said **made** any **sense**. At least it was over.

★ **pound** 무게의 단위 파운드. 60파운드는 약 27킬로그램이다.

He was the first one out the door when the bell rang.

"Theodore," came a voice from behind him, and then Tatiana's hand was on his arm.

"I thought your speech was really sweet."

"Yeah, well, I didn't have any stuffed animals, so I had to borrow one."

She smiled her **crooked** smile. "You were really nervous, weren't you?"

"Sort of, yeah."

"I could tell. Don't worry. You did a really good job. I'm going to vote for Coo."

He smiled. "Thanks. I mean, it doesn't matter to me, but it would make Ginny really happy if Coo won."

"Can I see it?"

"Sure." He handed the stuffed animal to Tatiana.

"What exactly is a coo?"

Armpit laughed. "I don't know, some kind of bunny-person-thingy.★"

Tatiana hugged Coo. "It feels so soft. I like the way you said Coo will give you courage, comfort, and strength."

He didn't **correct** her.

"Armpit! Hey, Armpit!"

X-Ray came **breezing** down the hall. "Armpit! I thought I'd never find you."

He greeted Tatiana with a "hey," then pulled a **wad** of

★ **thingy** 뭐더라. 이름을 모르거나 잊었을 때 쓰는 말.

money out of his pocket and started counting it. "Twenty, forty, sixty, eighty, one hundred." He handed Armpit a hundred dollars but wasn't finished yet.

"Twenty, forty, sixty, eighty, two hundred."

He was still not finished.

"Twenty, forty, sixty . . ."

Tatiana was no longer smiling. "I better go," she said, handing Coo back to Armpit.

"Uh, see you later," Armpit said to her, but she didn't turn around as she quickly walked away.

X-Ray counted out another hundred dollars. In total, X-Ray gave him five hundred and thirty dollars.

Armpit could hardly believe it. He had gotten **practically** all his money back. It was money he'd thought he'd never see again. "Was it the guys in the Suburban?"

"Those **clown**s? Hell★ no! A lady called me this morning. Wanted four tickets for her kid's birthday. The whole thing took twenty minutes. See, that's the way you do business. Not some **joker**s **string**ing you **along** like you're a yo-yo."

Armpit felt bad for having doubted X-Ray. "Wait a second," he said. "Four tickets should be five hundred and *forty*."

"Oh, yeah, I needed to borrow ten. You don't mind, do you?"

★ **hell** (속어) 제기랄.

10

It's a six-and-a-half-hour bus ride from Baton Rouge to Houston along I-10. Six buses and two trucks were making the **journey**. Kaira DeLeon's bus was **equip**ped with a flat-screen TV, a DVD player, two video game players, a **refrigerator**, a **microwave**, a treadmill,★ and a bathroom that included a shower as well as a **makeup** area. The only person on that bus, however, was the bus driver.

Kaira was sick of being alone and so had asked the guys in the band if she could ride with them. It was her first time on their bus and she knew her mother would **freak** if she found out. Her mother imagined all kinds of wild **goings-on** with a rock 'n' roll band, but all they were doing was playing cards. Tim B, the lead guitarist, had given her a beer, but she didn't like the taste and only took a few **sips** to be polite.

★ **treadmill** 트레드밀. 걷기나 달리기용 운동 기구로 우리나라에선 러닝머신이라고 부른다.

"Which way do we pass this time?" asked Duncan, a **bald** man with a **goatee**. He wore dark sunglasses, indoors or out. As far as Kaira could tell, all **bass** players always wore sunglasses.

"Left," said Cotton, the drummer, who then handed three cards to Kaira. Cotton was also bald, but that was because he **shave**d his head. Duncan still had hair on the sides.

"We passed left last time," said Billy Goat, whose last name was really Gotleib. He played keyboard.

"Too late, I already picked up my cards," said Cotton.

They may have been wild rock 'n' rollers at one time in their lives, but to Kaira they just seemed like a **bunch** of old men.

The Grateful Dead★ was playing over the sound system. She found the music **monotonous** but didn't **dare** say so out loud. That would have been **sacrilege** to these guys. She also **pretend**ed their **cigarette smoke** didn't **bother** her. Anything was better than another long ride alone.

She knew they all thought she was just a **spoil**ed prima donna✱ who didn't know anything about music. She'd heard them say as much. They'd been making music long before she was born, and often **mention**ed names of famous people they'd played with, names she'd never heard.

"Okay, who's got the two of clubs?❋" Kaira asked. "Oh, I do." She **giggle**d, then placed the card on the coffee table.

★ **Greatful Dead** 그레이트풀 대드. 미국의 록밴드.

✱ **prima donna** 프리마 돈나. 원래는 오페라의 주역 여가수라는 뜻이지만, 자기가 아주 중요한 인물인 줄 아는 변덕쟁이라는 뜻으로도 쓰인다.

❋ **club** 트럼프 카드의 클로버 무늬.

She had never played hearts★ with real people before, only on a computer, and was losing badly. It seemed like every hand she got **stuck** with the queen of spades.

The bus had two **couch**es set up at a right **angle**,✳ with a coffee table in the center "for drinks and feet." Those were Cotton's words. Just about everything he said made her laugh.

Three other band members and all three backup singers had missed the bus. They would have to find their own way to Houston.

"Goin' to Texas, we should listen to some Texas music," said Tim B. He stood up, then **stumble**d and fell against the side of the couch. Kaira didn't know if this was caused by the bus's movement or by what he'd been drinking.

"I'm all right," he said, **get**ting back **to his feet**, then made his way to the CD **rack**. "Hey, Kaira, you ever heard of Janis Joplin?❋"

Kaira **hesitate**d a moment, then said, "Oh, yeah, she really **rock**s!"

Cotton saw right through her. "You never heard of her, have you?"

"Uh, maybe, I'm not sure."

"If you heard her, you'd know," he said.

"We're talking real music," Tim B said as he **fumble**d with the CD. "**Raw** and to the bone."

★ **hearts** 카드 놀이의 일종.
✳ **right angle** 직각. 90도.
❋ **Janis Joplin** 제니스 조플린. 미국의 블루스 가수.

"And no cutesy-dootsy★ backup singers," said Duncan.

"I'll **drink to** that," said Cotton, **clink**ing beer bottles with him.

Kaira didn't like the backup singers any better than they did, but El Genius said they added sexual energy.

"Music needs **blank** spaces sometimes," Cotton said. "They **take up** all the blank spaces."

"Now you're talkin' about music," said Billy Goat. "Nobody makes real music anymore. It's all just a big show."

"Just background for MTV,✱" said Duncan. "It's almost impossible for a real musician to do anything **worth** listening to anymore. Now it's all I-don't-know-what."

"Don't listen to them, Kaira," said Cotton. "They been saying the same thing for the last twenty-five years."

Janis Joplin's voice came over the speakers. Kaira hadn't heard her before, but she liked her **right off**. Her **raspy** voice seemed to **drip** emotion. There was a kind of raw energy to the music, not like the **polish**ed songs she sang, in which every **note** was carefully planned and **orchestrate**d.

"Now, that's the way rock 'n' roll's supposed to be," said Tim B, half sitting down, half falling onto the couch.

"She's from Port Arthur, Texas," said Cotton.

"Where's that?"

None of the band members seemed to know.

★ **cutesy-dootsy** 깜찍한.
✱ **MTV** 미국 음악 채널.

"Somewhere in Texas," said Cotton.

Kaira laughed.

"So, Kaira," said Billy Goat. "I thought your mama didn't **allow** you to ride with us."

"She doesn't know I'm here," said Kaira. "Anyway, I got Fred to **protect** me from you dirty old men."

The Doofus was sitting up front next to the driver.

"Yeah, well, tell you what," said Billy Goat. "Your mama would **be** a lot **better off** if she kept her **watchful** eye on that husband of hers instead of on you."

"Don't go there," said Cotton.

"What do you mean by that?" asked Kaira.

"*Her watchful eye . . . ,*" sang Tim B.

"It's nothing," said Cotton.

"She's a grown girl," said Billy. "She **might as well** know the truth."

"You don't even know what you're talking about," said Cotton.

"What?" asked Kaira.

"All I'm saying," said Billy, "is your mama would be better off if she kept one eye on her husband and one eye on Aileen."

"And all I'm saying," said Cotton, "is when you don't know what you're talking about, you shouldn't talk so much."

"Aileen's my mom's friend," said Kaira. "They go shopping together."

"She's your dad's friend too," Tim B said with a laugh.

"He's not my dad," said Kaira.

"The girl likes to shop, I'll give you that," said Duncan. "But the question is this: whose money is she spending?"

Aileen was the person in **charge** of **coordinating** all the travel **arrange**ments for the tour. She had been the one who went and got **Pillow** when Kaira had left it behind in Connecticut. Kaira's father had given Pillow to her when she was three years old. When Aileen had called the hotel, the manager said they hadn't found any extra pillows, but Aileen didn't take no for an answer. She took a flight back to Connecticut, went to the hotel, and **personal**ly searched the **laundry** room until she found it.

Kaira didn't know what to think now. Aileen just seemed to be someone who really **had her act together**. So besides the fact that Aileen would be **betray**ing Kaira's mother, Kaira just couldn't imagine someone as smart and as cool as her being involved with someone as **gross** as El Genius.

Before Aileen started going along with Kaira's mother on her shopping **sprees**, Kaira's mother usually came home looking all **gaudy** and **ridiculous**. When Aileen went with her, the stuff she bought actually looked pretty good on her.

Aileen had good **taste**. At least in *clothes*.

Well, if El Genius really was **cheat**ing on her mother, then maybe that wasn't all bad, Kaira decided. Maybe her mom would **divorce** the freak!

She listened to Janis sing the **blues**, her voice filled with **suffer**ing, yet **tender**ness.

"Maybe we can meet Janis while we're in Texas?" she said.

Duncan and Tim B laughed.

"We'll all be meeting Janis someday," said Cotton. "But it won't be in Texas."

Janis had died of a drug **overdose** over forty years ago. She was only twenty-seven at the time.

"Hey, Kaira, ever hear of the Beatles?" asked Duncan.

"Who?" asked Kaira.

"You got to be **kid**din' me," said Duncan. "You're kidding me, right?"

Kaira **shrug**ged.

Cotton laughed. "She's playing with you, man."

Duncan wasn't so sure.

When they arrived at the hotel in Houston, Aileen was there to give them all their room keys and schedules. She had arrived earlier and had already gotten everybody checked in. They could just go right to their rooms. Their **luggage** would be brought up.

"You're Rhoda Morgenstern," she told Kaira as she handed her the key.

Kaira studied Aileen's face for some hint of **betrayal**, but her expression gave nothing away.

Even in her high heels, Aileen was shorter than Kaira. Everything about her was small: her waist, her feet, her ears, her mouth. She was stylish, **efficient**, and **compact**, like a cell phone.

"Do you know who Rhoda is?" Aileen asked.

"Mary Tyler Moore's best friend," said Kaira.

"Actually, Mary Richards's best friend," said Aileen.

It was a game they had. Aileen always **register**ed Kaira under an **assume**d name so she wouldn't be **hassle**d by fans. Aileen chose characters from old TV shows, but Kaira hadn't been **stump**ed yet.

She watched too much TV.

11

X-Ray picked up Armpit at school; then they drove to South **Congress** Avenue **in search of** a barbecue **joint** called Smokestack Lightnin'. Somebody by the name of Murdock wanted two tickets.

"I don't feel comfortable on someone else's **territory**," X-Ray had said.

"How come he couldn't meet you at the H-E-B?"

"Said he couldn't get away. Works from six in the morning until midnight."

Armpit thought that sounded a little **suspicious**.

So did X-Ray. That was why he wanted Armpit along.

"I got to be at work at one," Armpit **remind**ed him.

"I'll get you there," X-Ray **assure**d him.

Congress Avenue was called that because at its north end stood the **majestic** state capitol* building, with its **dome** and white **columns**. This was where the Texas congress met, but only every other year, so they couldn't cause too much damage.

Just south of the capitol was the **financial** and theater **district**, and then the Congress Street Bridge, which crossed over Town Lake. A **colony** of more than a million Mexican free-tailed bats✱ lived in the **cracks** and **crevices** on the underside of the bridge. Several **fancy** hotels lined the **bank**s of the lake—which actually was not a lake at all but a river—and tourists would gather at **sundown** to watch the bats **swarm** out from under the bridge as they went in search of food.

They **kept** the **mosquito population under control**.

"Is Murdock his first name or his last?" Armpit asked as they drove across the bridge.

A girl wearing very short pants and a bikini top was jogging with her dog.

"Whoo! Whoo!" X-Ray shouted through Armpit's open window.

The girl raised her middle finger.

South Congress Avenue hardly **resemble**d the street north of the river. Armpit looked out at **board**ed-up buildings, **liquor** stores, bars, and **tattoo parlor**s. At night the area would come alive with some of the best music in Austin, but in the heat and **glare** of the late-morning sun, it seemed as if the **entire** street **suffer**ed from a giant **hangover**.

"There it is," said X-Ray.

SMOKESTACK LIGHTNIN was painted in brown letters on

★ **state capitol** 미국 주(州)의회 의사당.
✱ **free-tailed bat** [동물] 긴꼬리박쥐.

the **smoky** glass of a **storefront** restaurant **located** next to the Fingernail **Emporium**. Armpit could smell the slow-cooked meat as soon as he stepped out of the car. If they hadn't been there to sell tickets, he wouldn't have minded a sausage wrap★ or a **chopped**-beef sandwich. He had missed lunch, thanks to X-Ray.

"Here, you better hold these," X-Ray said, handing Armpit the tickets.

He hadn't seen them since the day they bought them. Once again, he noticed *This ticket may not be resold* clearly printed on the back.

A bell on the door **jangled** as X-Ray pushed it open. Armpit followed him inside.

Only a couple of tables were **occupied**, but it wasn't noon yet. A roll of brown paper towels stood in the center of every table, along with **various** bottles of hot sauce.

They made their way to the front.

"What can I get you?" asked the man behind the counter. Various meats were on **display** behind a dirty glass window.

"We're looking for Murdock," said X-Ray.

"You found him."

He was a black man with gray hair and a gray **beard**. His **apron** was **splattered** with **grease** and barbecue sauce.

"X-Ray?"

"Yeah, and this is my partner, Armpit."

★ **sausage wrap** 얇게 구운 토르티야에 소시지와 채 썬 야채를 넣고 돌돌 말아 먹는 음식.

Murdock laughed at the name. "Armpit, huh? I used to know a **dude** who called himself Burnt Toast. He played the slide trombone.★ You play an **instrument**, Armpit?"

Armpit wanted to tell him about the **scorpion** but instead just shook his head.

"Let me see the tickets?"

Armpit felt a little worried as he handed the tickets over the glass case. There wasn't a whole lot they could do if Murdock decided just to keep them.

Murdock looked them over. "**Row** M. Not bad. Two hundred and seventy, right?"

"That's right," said X-Ray. "And you're getting a **bargain**."

"Well, I don't know about that," said Murdock. "But I only get to see my daughter one weekend a month, so I gotta **make the most of** it. When she heard Kaira DeLeon was going to be playing, it was all she could talk about. Hey, Wiley, you ever listen to Kaira DeLeon?"

"Who?" asked onc of the few customers in the place.

"Kaira DeLeon."

"Never heard a her."

Wiley wore a Harley✳ T-shirt and had tattoos up and down both arms.

"Go punch E-4," Murdock told him. "See if she don't **knock your socks off**." He turned his attention back to X-Ray.

★ **slide trombone** [악기] 슬라이드 트롬본. 가장 일반적으로 보급되어 있는 형태의 트롬본이다. U자광을 슬라이드시켜서 음의 높낮이를 조절한다.

✳ **Harley Davison** 미국의 대형 오토바이.

"I really do **appreciate** you boys coming all the way down here. When it's your own business, you got to stay on top of it twenty-four hours a day. I do it all: cook, wash dishes, **you name it.**"

Armpit was still waiting for either the money or Murdock to return the tickets.

Wiley **fumbled** with the jukebox.★ He was a big guy, and Armpit would not want to have to try to deal with him and Murdock.

"Can I get you something to eat?" Murdock asked. "**On the house.**"

"Chopped-beef sandwich," X-Ray answered right away.

"How 'bout you, Armpit?"

He was more concerned about the money than he was about food. "The same," he said.

"You like your sauce hot or **mild**?" Murdock asked.

"Mild," said X-Ray.

"Armpit?"

"The same."

Kaira's voice filled the restaurant.

I'm not the kinda✳ *girl who's* ***apt*** *to . . .*
Settle down.
No, I'm the kinda girl who likes to . . .

★ **jukebox** 주크박스. 요금을 넣고 원하는 곡을 들을 수 있는 기계.
✳ **kinda** kind of.

Get around.

Murdock brought the sandwiches over to the cash **register**. He opened it, then took out two hundred and seventy dollars, which he gave to X-Ray, along with his sandwich.

Armpit felt bad about not trusting him.

I see you lookin' at me
the way you do . . .
Just hold on!
a little longer.
Just hold on!
a little bit longer.
Hold on, baby
just a little bit longer
'Cause I'll get around to you!

Murdock laughed. "Man, don't you just love her?"

"She's all right," said Wiley.

"So what do you want to drink?" Murdock asked X-Ray.

Next to the cash register was a large metal **bucket** filled with ice and soft drinks.

"Root beer," said X-Ray.

Murdock looked at Armpit. "Let me guess. The same?"

Armpit **shrugg**ed.

"Does he tell you when to go to the bathroom, too?"

Armpit smiled and **sheepish**ly shrugged.

And now that you got me . . .
in your arms,
Ooh, I feel so . . .
soft and warm.
There's only one thing
I want to say . . .

Armpit bit into his sandwich. He'd eaten a lot of barbecue in his life, but this might have been the very best. Of course, that might have **had something to do with** the fact that he now had all his money back, and then some.

Just hold on!
a little longer.
Just hold on!
a little bit longer.
Hold on, baby,
just a little bit longer
And then I'll be on my way.

12

X-Ray sold four more tickets to a couple of high school students from Westlake, and just like that, Armpit had another two hundred and seventy dollars. He was up three hundred dollars, and there were still two tickets left, which would mean another hundred and thirty-five for him.

The final two ruler-of-the-world campaign speeches were given Thursday morning. The second-to-last speech was given by Claire, Tatiana's friend, who brought Dumbo the Elephant.

". . . so all the other elephants **made fun of** him, but then he got drunk and **ended up** in a tree, and these birds sang to him. And then his mouse friend said he could fly because of a magic **feather**. . . ."

"Yeah, I've seen the movie," a boy in back said, but Claire just continued.

"I used to love that movie!" Armpit heard Tatiana **whisper**. He wondered if she still planned to **vote** for Coo.

The last speech, given by Robbie Kinkaid, was for an armadillo★ name Joe. Robbie **obvious**ly made up the speech as he went along, including the name of his armadillo.

"This is an armadillo, I think. You can vote for him if you want. His name is . . . Joe. Joe the Armadillo. He's brown, and has four legs, and this **shell** thingy. . . ."

Then came the vote.

Everyone had to write down his or her first and second choices.

Joe the Armadillo won, and Dumbo was **elect**ed **vice** ruler of the world. If for any reason Joe was unable to **fulfill** his **obligation**s, Dumbo would **take over**.

Armpit tried not to let his disappointment show. After all, it was just a stupid **assignment**, and people just voted for the only ones they could remember.

"I'm sorry Coo didn't win," Tatiana said to him after class. She placed her hand on his arm as she said it.

"No **biggie**."

"You gave the best speech," she told him, her hand still there.

"It would have made Ginny happy."

"She's your sister?"

"My neighbor."

"That's right. She has leukemia?"

"Cerebral palsy."

★ **armadillo** [동물] 아르마딜로. 아메리카 대륙에 사는 가죽이 딱딱한 포유류.

Armpit wondered if Tatiana had forgotten her hand was there, but if she had, he wasn't about to remind her. Her fingernails were painted green. Her **perfume** smelled like cantaloupe.★

"Say, listen," he said. "Do you like Kaira DeLeon?"

She **squeezed** his arm. "'Red **Alert**!' I love that song."

"You want to go to the concert on Saturday?"

She bit her lip. "You mean with you?"

"Yeah."

"Yeah."

"Yeah?" he asked, just to make sure.

She smiled. "Yeah."

By the time **economics** was over, Armpit had **convinced** himself that X-Ray had already sold the last two tickets and that he was going to have to buy two from a **scalper** for fifteen hundred dollars. He could hear X-Ray's voice in his head. "Seven hundred and fifty dollars—*each*."

When the bell rang he **bolted** out of his seat and hurried to the office, where he asked the **secretary** if he could use the phone. She seemed **sympathetic**, but it was against school **policy**. **Apparently** not the **principal**, the **superintendent**, or even the president of the United States could change school policy.

Where was Joe the Armadillo when you needed him?

He left the office and **spotted** Matt Kapok, a **skinny** white

---

★ **cantaloupe** [식물] 칸탈루프. 껍질은 녹색에 과육은 오렌지색인 멜론.

guy from his economics class. Matt was probably the only student in his class who was taking summer school because he wanted to, not because he had to.

"Matt!" Armpit shouted as he **charge**d toward him. "You got fifty cents? I'm **desperate**, man!"

Matt backed up against a row of **locker**s as he took his wallet out of his back pocket. "Uh, sure. Here." He held out a dollar, but it dropped out of his hand before Armpit could take it.

As Armpit bent down to pick it up, Matt **sidestep**ped him and quickly disappeared around the corner.

"I'll pay you back!" Armpit called after him, but didn't know if Matt heard him.

He went back to the office, where the secretary gave him four quarters for the dollar, then went to the pay phone★ and called X-Ray.

"You sell the last two tickets?"

"Not to worry, not to worry," X-Ray said in a **soothing** voice.

"Have you sold them!"

"Look, you got to—"

"Yes or no?"

"Not yet, but—"

"Don't!"

"Wait a second. Who are you, and what have you done with

★ pay phone 동전을 넣는 공중 전화.

Armpit?"

Armpit told him about Tatiana. "She had her hand on my arm, and with her perfume and everything, I couldn't think straight."

"Was she the one I saw you talkin' to that time? Strange hair, **goofy** smile?"

"Yeah."

"She's pretty cute."

"I'll pay you a hundred and thirty-five for the two tickets," said Armpit. "That woulda been your **share** if you sold them."

A hundred and thirty-five seemed like a **bargain**. He was **relieved** not to have to pay fifteen hundred.

"Man, that girl's really **gotten to you**," said X-Ray. "Look, they're your tickets. You don't have to buy them twice!" He laughed. "That musta* been some perfume!"

---

* **musta** must have.

13

"Well, that's the way it goes," Ginny said when Armpit told her that Coo didn't win. They were taking their daily walk around the **block**.

"What they should have done," said Armpit, "is write down all the **candidates**' names on a **ballot**. The problem was nobody remembered any of the speeches."

"Well, that's the way it goes," Ginny said again.

Her face **twitch**ed as she said it, and Armpit didn't know if that was **due** to her **disability** or if she was trying not to cry.

"But hey, I got an A on my speech," he said. "Thanks to Coo." He smiled. "Of course, it doesn't hurt that Coach Simmons thinks I'll be going out for football."

"Like how Mrs. R-Randsinkle g-gave m-me an A in art," said Ginny.

Mrs. Randsinkle had been her teacher last year.

"And I c-c-couldn't even c-c-color inside the l-lines."

Armpit noticed that Ginny **stutter**ed more when she talked about school.

"Well, you know, art's not just about coloring in the lines," said Armpit. "It's about **creativity**. Putting your **soul** on the paper. You're good at that."

"No, she just felt sorry for me. She w-w-wished I w-wasn't in her class. She's afraid of my s-**seizures**."

Armpit would have liked to tell her that wasn't true, but he knew it probably was. Ginny had enough problems without him telling her she was wrong. "Well, they are kind of scary," he said. "But I **bet** there's a lot she liked about you too. You're a very **thoughtful** and **caring** person."

Ginny's arm was raised, but this time she noticed it herself and lowered it.

"Oh, I didn't tell you! I asked a girl to go to the Kaira DeLeon concert with me."

Ginny covered her **gaping** mouth with her hand. From behind it, she asked, "What'd she say?"

"She said yeah."

Ginny **giggle**d.

"What's so funny?"

"The w-way y-you l-look."

"How do I look?"

"All **dreamy**-eyed." She giggled some more. "What's her name?" she asked in a **teasing** kind of voice.

"Tatiana."

Ginny giggled.

"What?"

"The way you said it."

"How did I say it?"

"Tati-*ahna*."

"Tatiana," said Armpit, trying to sound **normal**.

"Tati-*ahna*," said Ginny. "Is she pretty?"

"Yeah, but in a different kind of way. It's like that Kaira DeLeon song '**Imperfection**'? You know?" He sang: "*You **reflect** on your reflection. But you will never see. Your imperfection is your finest **quality**.*"

Ginny laughed. He wasn't a very good singer.

"She's cute because of all her imperfections," Armpit explained.

"I knew it!" said Ginny. "I smelled her p-**perfume** on Coo."

Armpit remembered Tatiana had hugged Coo.

"Tati-*ahna*," teased Ginny.

"I don't even know if she really likes me," Armpit said. "I think she's just a big Kaira DeLeon fan."

"She likes you," said Ginny.

"Oh, yeah? How do you know?"

"Because. You're a v-very thoughtful and caring p-person."

While Ginny and Armpit were walking around the block, Tatiana was sitting on the floor of Claire's bedroom, along with their friend Roxanne. They were sharing a bowl of popcorn and drinking diet **sodas**.★

★ **diet soda** 칼로리가 낮은 탄산 음료.

"Aren't you just a little bit scared?" Roxanne asked.

"No, why should I be?"

Claire and Roxanne looked at each other **knowing**ly.

"He is kind of dangerous," said Claire.

"Maybe that's what she likes about him," said Roxanne. "The *danger!*"

"He's a nice guy," said Tatiana. "He's sweet."

"Sweet? He almost *killed* two people, girl!" Roxanne **remind**ed her.

"Do you know what they called him at Camp Green Lake?" asked Claire.

"Yes, I know," said Tatiana.

"Armpit!" Claire said. "Out of all those **nasty**, **sweaty** guys, he smelled the worst!"

"It was so bad, even the other sweaty guys noticed," said Roxanne. "And you know *guys!* It's gotta **stink** really bad before they notice."

"And you really want to sit next to him, in that hot **arena**, with everyone all **jam**med close together?" asked Claire.

"He'll probably put his big, fat, sweaty arm around you," said Roxanne.

"I like 'Red Alert!'" said Tatiana. "I think it'll be cool to see Kaira DeLeon sing it **in person**."

Armpit stopped in the restroom before school on Friday and **splash**ed his face with cold water. Then he **caught up** with Tatiana just before she got to class.

"My friend said I could use his car. One of the doors doesn't open, but at least I got wheels.★"

"That's great," said Tatiana without looking at him. She entered the classroom and **maneuver**ed her way between the desks. Claire whispered something to her when she sat down, and Tatiana said something back.

Armpit couldn't hear what they said, but he was able to read Tatiana's lips. She told Claire to shut up.

He went to work early on Saturday, glad to be doing **physical labor** so he wouldn't drive himself crazy thinking about the concert and Tatiana. Hernandez **dump**ed a **truckload** of **dirt** in the driveway, and now they mixed it with peat moss✻ before spreading it around the yard.

Better to use a fifty-cent plant and ten-dollar dirt than a ten-dollar plant and fifty-cent dirt. Jack Dunlevy said that all the time.

He got home around four-thirty but didn't shower right away, or else he'd be all sweaty again by the time he picked up Tatiana. Instead, he went over to Ginny's.

Ginny's mother looked all **frazzle**d when she opened the door. "Oh, Theodore, I'm so glad you're here," she said. "Ginny's— It's my fault. I said something I shouldn't have."

Armpit stepped inside. "Ginny, are you okay?"

★ **wheel** '바퀴'라는 뜻이 '바퀴 모양의 것', '바퀴 모양의 기구'로 확대되어 '자전거'나 '자동차'를 일컫는 의미로 쓰인다.

✻ **peat moss** 초탄(草炭). 일반 토양과 섞어 원예에 사용한다.

She sat on the floor, crying while she hugged Coo.

"Ginny, what's wrong?"

"My d-d-dad . . ." She was unable to continue.

"Did your dad call?"

Her father had left home when she was a baby.

"He l-left because of m-me. B-because of my disa-b-b-bility."

"That's not what I said!" said her mother.

"It's true!" Ginny **exclaim**ed.

"It wasn't you. It was the whole situation."

"If I g-get b-b-better, will he c-come h-h-home?"

Ginny's mom was crying now too.

Armpit sat on the floor next to Ginny. "I didn't know your dad was **disable**d," he said.

"He's n-not."

"Sounds like he is. He's a lot **worse off** than you are. You just had a little bleeding in your brain. He's got something wrong with his soul. I mean, if he left your mom and you, man, there's got to be something really wrong with him."

Ginny **shrug**ged.

"I sure hope he gets better. You at least can go to physical **therapy**. I don't know what they can do for someone with no heart and soul."

There was a knock on the door; then it opened, and Armpit's mother **lean**ed her head in. "Is Theodore here?" She had the telephone with her, her hand covering the **mouthpiece**. "It's *her*."

His mother was almost as excited about his date as he was, even though he kept telling her it wasn't a *date*. They were just going to **hang out** at the concert together.

He took the phone and walked outside for **privacy**. "Hello?"

"Hi, how's it goin'?" asked Tatiana.

"Great. I'm really looking forward to the concert."

"Look, I don't know how to say it. I'm not good at this."

"At what?"

"I'm really sorry, but I can't go to the concert."

He didn't respond.

"Theodore? You there?"

"Yeah."

"I'm really sorry. There's this family thing I got to do. I forgot all about it. They won't let me out of it. My parents have this thing about *family time!*"

"I understand," said Armpit.

"You sure?"

"Yeah."

"But I want you to tell me all about it on Monday, okay?"

"Sure."

"Promise? Every song she sings. What clothes she's wearing. I want to know *everything!*"

"Okay."

"I really feel bad about this. Maybe you can find someone else to go with you."

"Yeah, don't worry about it."

He **hung up**, then **dial**ed X-Ray's number.

"Was it Tati-*ahna?*" Ginny teased when he returned to her house. She seemed to be feeling better.

"She can't go to the concert."

"Oh, I'm so sorry," her mother said.

"Well, that's the way it goes," Armpit said. He winked at Ginny.

"You want to hold Coo?" she **offer**ed.

He shook his head. X-Ray had said people were still calling about the tickets, so maybe it wasn't too late. If nothing else, they could go to the Lonestar and try to sell them at the door.

But now another thought came to him. "So, Ginny," he said. "You want to go to the concert with me?"

Her eyes **widen**ed. She looked to her mother, who shrugged, then **nod**ded her **approval**.

14

"Just don't come home with your nose **pierced**," Ginny's mother told her.

Ginny promised she wouldn't.

Armpit's parents seemed more worried about Ginny's safety than her own mother, but Armpit had a lot to do with that since his natural response was to **argue** with anything they said.

"Now, you keep a sharp eye on Ginny at all times."

"She can take care of herself."

"There are a lot of crazy people at a rock concert."

"Just because people have **tattoo**s or pierced **tongue**s doesn't mean they're crazy!"

"If you're not going to be **responsible** . . ."

"Ginny's mother trusts me. Why can't my own parents?"

"Because we know you."

He didn't know why he argued with them like that. He was just as concerned as they were, if not more so. He knew a rock concert could be a wild **scene** and had every **intention** of **protect**ing Ginny and holding her hand until they were safely in their seats.

He called X-Ray to make sure he hadn't already sold the tickets.

"I got a guy on the **line** right now!" X-Ray said. "He said he'd pay a hundred and fifty a ticket. I told you the price would only go up. Didn't I tell you?"

"You can't sell them. I'm taking Ginny."

"Ginny? Are you **outta★ your gourd**? Have you completely lost your mind?"

"Look, she had a really bad day. Just bring the tickets over here. I want to get an early start so we can **beat** the crowds."

"We're talking three hundred dollars!"

"I promised Ginny."

X-Ray said he'd be over in twenty minutes, but he did not sound happy about it.

Armpit **sigh**ed as he set the phone back in its **cradle**. Maybe he was crazy. He didn't even know if Ginny would be able to **handle** the loud music and the crowds.

The phone rang a moment later. It was X-Ray again.

"I told the guy they were no longer for sale, and he offered two hundred a ticket."

"No," said Armpit.

"Four hundred dollars!"

★ outta out of.

"No."

It was almost seven o'clock. X-Ray still hadn't showed. Armpit and Ginny waited on the front **porch**, along with Ginny's mother.

"You listen to Theodore and do everything he tells you," said her mother.

"I will," Ginny promised.

He would be driving Ginny's mother's car. She **insist**ed on it, which was fine with him, because if he took the X-Mobile they'd have to first take X-Ray home and they were **run**ning **out of** time. Besides, Ginny's mother's Camry★ was **undoubted**ly more **reliable**, and safer, than X-Ray's machine.

His mother came outside. "Still not here?"

Armpit shook his head.

"You must be very proud of Theodore," said Ginny's mother.

Armpit's mother was **caught off guard**. "Uh, well, yes, of course I am."

If he sold those tickets I'm going to kill him, Armpit thought, and then a second later the X-Mobile pulled around the corner.

X-Ray parked in front and slid out the **passenger** side as Armpit and Ginny headed down to meet him.

"What took you so long?" Armpit demanded.

X-Ray **ignore**d the question. "Hey, Ginny, are you ready to

★ Camry 토요타(Toyota)사에서 나오는 차.

rock 'n' roll?"

"Yes."

X-Ray laughed, then handed Armpit the **envelope** containing the two remaining tickets. "Just remember," he said. "Be **flexible.**"

"All right," said Armpit.

"You hear what I'm saying? *Flexible.*"

"Yeah, I hear you," Armpit said. He didn't have time for any of X-Ray's **nonsense.**

He and Ginny got into her mother's car; then he carefully backed it out of the driveway while everyone waved good-bye. He saw X-Ray say something to Ginny's mother, who laughed.

They turned the corner. The clock on the **dashboard** read 7:06. The concert wasn't until eight.

He winked at Ginny. She shut and opened both eyes.

Armpit sang: "*I'm gonna take you for a ride! And we're gonna have some fun! I'm gonna take you for a ride!*"

Ginny joined in: "*And we're gonna have some fun!*"

Armpit: "*I'm gonna take you someplace you never been before . . .*"

They sang the last line together. "*And you'll never be the same again!*"

15

They sang all the way to the Lonestar **Arena**. "You know, you don't **stutter** at all when you sing," Armpit **point**ed **out**.

Ginny laughed.

"Maybe you should sing all the time."

Ginny laughed again. "*Good mor-ning,*" she sang. "*I'll have pan-cakes.*"

Armpit laughed as he **pull**ed **into** the parking lot, which was **cram**med with cars and people.

Ginny sang, "*Two plus two is four, Mrs. Randsinkle.*"

He couldn't find anything that **resemble**d a parking space. It was X-Ray's fault for being so late.

He lifted the **handicapped placard** out of the pocket in the door beside him. "I'm going to have to use this," he said.

Ginny stopped singing.

"It's not because I don't think you can walk."

Ginny **nod**ded. "I know," she said.

He **hung** the placard on the **rearview mirror** and parked right in front.

Ginny tightly held Armpit's hand as they made their way to the building. She was so excited she would have fallen several times if he hadn't been holding her up. "Small steps," he **remind**ed her.

"Is she all right?" the ticket taker asked.

"She's dancing," Armpit told him.

Inside, they had to **maneuver** their way through **throng**s of people all moving in different directions. Before going to their seats, they got in a long line at one of the **concession** counters. Ginny's mother had given her twenty dollars.

Armpit lifted Ginny up on his shoulders so she could see. She really wanted to get a Kaira DeLeon **official** tour T-shirt, but when they got to the front, they were told it cost twenty-eight dollars.

Armpit was willing to pay the other eight dollars, plus **tax**, but Ginny's mother had told her not to let Theodore pay for anything. Instead, Ginny bought two soft drinks,★ which came in plastic **souvenir** cups, and a **bucket** of popcorn for them to share. She paid with her twenty-dollar bill and got one dollar and seventy-five cents back in change.

Armpit held the popcorn and his drink, while Ginny held on to her drink and his arm, as they slowly made their way to their seats. He couldn't help thinking about the last

---

★ **soft drink** 탄산이 주입된 청량 음료.

time he'd held a bucket of popcorn in a crowded place, but they safely reached **section** B, **row** M, seats 1 and 2 without **incident**.

The large stage, with giant towers of speakers on either side, **jut**ted out in front of them. Behind them were at least forty rows of seats, and those were the good seats. Beyond those, and to the sides, were two **tier**s of **bleacher**s.

He **glance**d around at the people seated nearby, realizing they were the ones to whom X-Ray sold the tickets. Well, at least they got their money's **worth**. These really were great seats.

"Great seats, huh?" he said.

"Yes," said Ginny.

He looked for Murdock but didn't see him. An African American girl was sitting a few seats away with her boyfriend. If she was Murdock's daughter, then that was too bad. He remembered Murdock had bought the tickets so he could spend time with his daughter on the one weekend a month he got to see her.

Backstage, Kaira DeLeon was **chew**ing a piece of gum that had long lost its **flavor**. This was always the worst time for her. She knew she'd be all right once she started singing. Then she would disappear into the music.

The backstage area was filled with people, half of whom she didn't **recognize**. Besides all the people working on tour, there were record company **executive**s, friends of record company executives, children of lawyers, brothers-in-law★ of **security personnel**. Every once in a while someone managed to **slip** past the Doofus and ask for her **autograph**. In Houston, a woman and her two kids had actually asked her to sing a song for them.

Kaira wore a lavender sweat suit.✢ Beneath it was the **outfit** she'd wear for the show, which was little more than **sparkling** underwear with **fringe**. For some reason it seemed all right to dress that way in front of thousands of people, but in this small area it would have been **embarrass**ing.

She wished she had stayed in her dressing room instead of having to be around all these people. It was almost eight, but the concerts never started **on time**. She should know that by now. El Genius liked to "make 'em wait." He didn't want her taking the stage until the audience had worked itself into a **frenzy**.

She looked at him, shouting into his walkie-talkie.❋ She **pitied** the person on the other end. Next to him, her mother was drinking from one of those **horrible** plastic souvenir cups with her picture on it. **Lately** her mother had begun having cocktails during the show.

At least Aileen wasn't around. Kaira could no longer **stand** the sight of her. She'd already gone to Dallas to make sure all the **arrange**ments had been taken care of at their next hotel.

Kaira wondered if her mother **suspect**ed there was

★ **brother-in-law** 매부, 매형, 처남, 형부 등 혈연이 아니라 결혼으로 생긴 형제를 말한다.
✢ **sweat suit** 운동 경기자가 추위를 막기 위해 경기 전후에 입는 상·하의.
❋ **walkie-talkie** 워키토키. 휴대용 소형 무선 송수신기를 말한다.

something going on between Jerome and Aileen. Maybe that was the reason for the cocktails.

A local DJ was **onstage** now, **firing up** the crowd.

"Is everyone ready?"

ᘓ

"Yes!" Ginny shouted **at the top of her lungs**, but even Armpit, sitting right next to her, couldn't hear her for the crowd.

"Are you sure?"

"Yes!" he and Ginny shouted.

"Because Kaira DeLeon will be standing on this ***very spot*** *in just five minutes!"*

Armpit felt Ginny's fingernails dig into his arm.

"So just hold on a little longer!"

Everyone **cheer**ed the line from one of Kaira's songs.

Armpit only slowly became **aware** that somebody was **tap**ping his shoulder. He turned to see a security guard.

"Excuse me," the guard said, **apparent**ly not for the first time. "May I see your tickets, please?"

A man and young girl stood behind him. The girl was probably Ginny's age, although she was much bigger.

"May I see your tickets, please?" the security guard asked again.

"My tickets?"

"Please."

Armpit tried to remember what he'd done with them. He

hoped he hadn't dropped them when he was dealing with the popcorn and **soda**.

"You're sitting in our seats!" the girl **accused**.

"Are n-n-not!" said Ginny.

Armpit stood up to check his pockets. The security guard **instinctive**ly stepped back from him.

"I don't want any trouble," the guard said, placing a hand on his walkie-talkie. "I just want to make sure you're in your right seats."

Armpit didn't want any trouble either. "I got them here somewhere."

"I'm going to have to ask you to come with me, Sir."

"I've got the tickets!" Armpit shouted, partly out of **frustration** and partly to be heard over the crowd, which was now **stomp**ing their feet with **impatience**.

"Please come with me, sir, and I'll help you find your **correct** seats."

"Just wait!"

The guard spoke into his walkie-talkie. "I'm going to need some help here. Section B."

Armpit's pants had too many pockets: three on the right front, two on the left front, and two in the back. "Found 'em!" he **exclaim**ed. They were in one of the front pockets. He handed the **stub**s to the security guard.

As the guard was looking them over, two uniformed police officers hurried quickly down the **aisle**. "What's the problem here?" asked one of the officers.

"No problem," said Armpit.

"**Counterfeit** tickets," said the security guard. "He **refuses** to leave."

"What?" Armpit exclaimed, reaching for the tickets. "Let me see . . ."

An officer **grab**bed his arm and **twist**ed it behind his back, **spin**ning him around.

Armpit **jerk**ed himself free, but the other officer grabbed him.

The next thing he knew he was on the floor, his face pressed against the concrete. He could feel a knee digging into the small of his back.

It felt like his arms were being **rip**ped out of their **socket**s as first one, then the other was jerked behind his back. Then they were **handcuff**ed together.

His head was lifted off the floor by his hair and a police officer shouted in his face. "What's she on?★"

"What'd you give her?" shouted the other officer.

He **wince**d in pain. It felt like his hair was about to be ripped right out of his head. He could hear the security guard calling for a doctor. "We're going to have to **pump her stomach**!"

The officer **abrupt**ly let go of his hair, and his face **bang**ed against the floor. "Look," the officer said, no longer shouting. "It would really help for us to know what kind of drugs we're dealing with here."

★ **What's she on?** 무슨 마약을 한 거야?

"You think it's bad now," said the other one. "Believe me, you do not want anything to happen to her."

"Help us save her life!"

"What's she on!"

Armpit managed to get a **glimpse** of Ginny, her body jerking around uncontrollably on the floor.

The sight of her made him **lurch** up, knocking both officers backward, but just for a moment. They quickly **tackle**d him again, and then a **billy club slam**med against the side of his neck.

"What's going on here?"

It was a woman's voice.

"Stay back, **Mayor**, he's all **whack**ed out on something."

"You don't hit somebody who's already on the ground, in handcuffs," said Cherry Lane.

"He drugged that little girl."

"She's not on drugs!" Armpit **gasp**ed.

"Shut up!" said the officer, pushing his head against the floor.

He managed to raise his face back up. "I dug a **trench** at your house!" he gasped. "You said you **admire**d me!"

The mayor **lean**ed down with her hands on her knees to get a better look at him. Her long silver hair hung on both sides of her face. "You work for Jack Dunlevy?"

"Yes!"

"What's wrong with the girl?"

"She's not on drugs. I **swear**. She's having a **seizure**."

"He was caught with counterfeit tickets," said one of the officers.

"Let me help her," Armpit **plead**ed. "Please."

"You think *he knew* they were counterfeit?" asked the mayor. "You think he'd sit in those seats if he knew they were counterfeit?"

"I can help her," said Armpit.

"Let him go!" ordered the mayor.

"I don't think that's a good idea."

"You let him go right now, unless you want to spend the next ten years walking up and down Lamar Boulevard."

The officer twisted Armpit's arm extra hard as he unlocked the handcuffs. The other officer was ready with his **baton**.

Staying low, Armpit hurried to Ginny. **Drool drip**ped from her mouth as her body **writhe**d and **twitch**ed. Her eyes were wide open, but they weren't seeing anything.

The floor was **sticky** with **spill**ed drinks and popcorn.

"I'm here now, Ginny," he said softly. "I'm here now." He wiped the drool off her face and **adjust**ed her glasses, which had fallen to one side.

The people and their chairs had been cleared from the area.

"Is she going to be all right?" asked the mayor.

He slipped his hand below her head, then gently lifted her up off the floor. "It's okay now," he **whisper**ed. He held her **trembling** body against his chest.

"Now what?" Kaira demanded. There had been some kind of

disturbance out on the floor and the waiting was driving her crazy.

"Funniest thing I ever saw!" laughed Jerome Paisley as he returned to the backstage area. "This little bit of a girl, **wriggling** around on the floor, drooling all over herself. She looked like a goldfish that fell out of its bowl. You know how they **flop** around until they die?"

"You think that's *funny?*" asked Kaira.

"The thing is, everyone thinks she's on drugs, right? But she's not. She was born **spastic**!"

"And that's *funny?*" asked Kaira again.

"How **awful**," Kaira's mother said, although she seemed more concerned with her drink, which was now down to nothing but ice.

"See, she was with this big black **dude**," El Genius explained. "The **cops** are beating the **crap** out of him while the little white girl was having a **spaz** attack, because they thought he gave her drugs!"

"Oh, yeah, that's really funny!" said Kaira. God, she hated him!

"He meant **unusual** funny, not ha-ha funny," explained her mother.

"That's not how he said it."

"It was their own fault," said her mother's husband. "They paid like three hundred dollars to some **scalper** for counterfeit tickets!" He laughed. "Some people are too stupid to live!"

"Where are they now?" asked Kaira.

"They should have the area cleared and cleaned up in about five or ten minutes. You better have Rosemary do some **touch-up** on your hair. It looks a little flat."

"Where are they now?" Kaira asked again.

They were on a **cot** in the security area, **surround**ed by a half-dozen security and medical personnel. Armpit still held Ginny in his arms, but her attack had **subside**d into tears and **hiccups**.

The medical personnel were trained to **handle** drug **overdose**s and **minor** injuries, and knew very little about cerebral palsy.

"She doesn't need to go to the hospital," Armpit said. "She just needs space to breathe."

A woman put her hand on Ginny's **wrist**. "I'm just going to take your **pulse**."

Ginny jerked her hand away.

The mayor also was there, despite repeated suggestions by the head of security that she return to her seat and enjoy the show. Out in the arena the crowd was calling for Kaira and stomping their feet. Armpit could feel the **vibration**s on the floor.

"You say he came at you?" the officer in **charge** asked one of the officers who handcuffed Armpit.

"I was reaching for the ticket!" Armpit tried to explain, then felt Ginny tremble at his sudden **outburst**.

"He made a **threaten**ing movement, but I was able to quickly gain control of the situation."

"There's no question he was **resisting arrest**," said the other officer.

"His friend was having a seizure!" the mayor pointed out. "He only wanted to help her!"

"Please, Mayor. It would be better for everyone if you returned to your seat."

"I'm not going to let you **justify** your actions by **blaming** the **victim**," the mayor said **firm**ly. "Let me ask you something," she said, directing her attention to the officer. "Would the gesture have been so threatening if he was white?"

Armpit **had to hand it to** Cherry Lane. She was one tough lady.

"Instead of **persecuting** the victim," the mayor went on, "you should be back out there, getting the names and phone numbers of everyone seated in that area. Somebody else may have bought tickets from the same scalper."

Two more people entered the room: a gum-chewing African American teenage girl wearing a lavender sweat suit, followed by a thirty-year-old well-dressed white guy.

"Who the hell are you?" demanded the head of security.

Ginny knew who she was. Her **sobs** instantly **cease**d.

"I heard there was a problem with some tickets," the girl said. She sat on the cot next to Armpit and asked Ginny her name.

"Ginny."

"Hi, Ginny."

"Hi, Kaira," said Ginny.

When Armpit realized who she was, he couldn't believe she was sitting right next to him, her leg almost touching his.

"Are you feeling better?" Kaira asked.

"Yes."

"Is she going to be okay?" Kaira asked Armpit.

"She's fine!" Armpit said, sounding a little too **enthusiastic**. He couldn't believe he was talking to her. "It's happened before. She just needs a little time and space."

"I hear that," Kaira said to Ginny. "It's a **madhouse** out there. All these people crowded around, and then they tell you your tickets are no good."

"My body w-went to red **alert**," said Ginny.

That made Kaira smile. "You seem okay now," she said. "Would you like to come backstage and watch the concert from there?"

"Yes."

16

Armpit wasn't certain if Kaira's invitation included him as well, but he wasn't about to be left behind. Kaira led them out of the security area and down a dark hallway.

"Sorry I walk so slow," said Ginny.

"There's no hurry," said Kaira, as out in the **arena** the audience was **stomp**ing and **clap**ping.

"So are you like her nurse or something?" she asked Armpit.

"We're just friends, that's all," he told her.

"He's my best friend," said Ginny.

"I'm so sorry!" Kaira said. Because Ginny was a white girl, and Armpit was older and an African American, she had just **assume**d he worked for her family. *Talk about racism!*

Armpit had no idea what she was sorry for.

"This is Fred, my bodyguard," Kaira said. "He's here to **protect** me from Ginny. You think you can **handle** her, Fred? She looks **awful**ly dangerous."

Armpit smiled at the joke, but he and everyone else knew Ginny wasn't the one Fred was closely watching.

"Just doin' my job, Miss DeLeon," said Fred.

They reached a **flight** of stairs and Kaira asked Ginny if she could make it up by herself.

"I need to hold on to someone."

"Hold on to me," said Kaira, **extend**ing her hand.

Armpit was amazed by Ginny's calmness. She didn't seem one bit nervous around Kaira DeLeon. He, **on the other hand**, could hardly think straight.

Kaira led them up a flight of stairs, then through a door and into the backstage area. Several people hurried toward them.

"These are my friends," Kaira said. "Ginny, and . . ."

"Theodore," said Armpit, helping her out.

"We need to set them up somewhere they can see the show." She turned back to Armpit and Ginny. "David will take care of you."

David wore a vest but no shirt. He had red hair, a red **beard**, and a red hairy chest. Tools of **various** sorts were **attach**ed to his belt and in the many pockets of his vest.

"Come with me," David said as a Hispanic★ woman led Kaira away. "We'll set you up behind the soundboard.✱"

"Wait, wait, wait," said a very pretty woman in a short skirt and tight T-shirt. "Hold on, honey. Let me get you cleaned up

---

★ **Hispanic** 히스패닉. 라틴 아메리카계의 사람.
✱ **soundboard** (= sounding board) 무대 위나 스피커의 뒤에 설치하는 반향판.

first. David, get them some T-shirts."

The woman introduced herself as Rosemary and brought them to a **makeup** area, where the three backup singers were **smoking**.

While she was helping Ginny wash up, David returned with a box of **souvenir** T-shirts. "What color you want?"

"Red," said Ginny.

"One for him, too," said Rosemary, indicating Armpit.

"I'm fine," said Armpit.

"You're a **mess**. Now take off your shirt."

David **grab**bed a couple of folding chairs and led Armpit and Ginny out onto the stage. He walked close enough to the keyboard that he could have played a **note**.

The audience, which had been **yell**ing and stomping **impatient**ly, suddenly stopped and **applaud**ed, glad that at last something was happening.

Ginny **squeeze**d Armpit's hand.

David set up the chairs behind a large piece of electronic **equip**ment. "Don't worry," he said. "You'll be in**visible** here."

They were near one of the speaker towers,★ but back behind it, so they wouldn't be **blast**ed by the sound.

The soundboard **operator** introduced himself as Terry. He wore headphones. The soundboard **consist**ed of a **panel** of switches, **dials**, and lights. "This is so the band members can

★ **speaker tower** 음향 신호탑.

hear themselves and each other," he explained.

"Cool," said Armpit.

David returned a moment later with two souvenir cups filled with lemon-lime **soda**. He hurried off just as everything went **pitch dark**, and then the music shook the stage, nearly knocking Armpit out of his chair.

Strobe lights★ flashed on the various band members, and then a green **spotlight** settled on Kaira DeLeon.

"You've heard she's ***naughty****,*
You've heard she's wild.
You've heard she's just
A sweet ***innocent*** *child!*

"Well, now's the chance
for you to find out!
'Cause I'm the she
You been hearin' about!"

It was hard to imagine that this was the same gum-**chew**ing girl he had just met a few minutes earlier. She was **dazzling**ly beautiful.

"You wake up screaming
In the middle of the night

★ **strobe light** 깜빡임을 방지하기 위해 설계된 조명 장치의 일종.

*Was it a **nightmare?***
*Or was it too much **delight?**"*

The floor beneath him **bounced** with each **beat** of the drum, and he could feel the **bass vibrating** right down to his bones. He hoped it wasn't too loud for Ginny, but she just stared at Kaira DeLeon, **mesmerized**.

"Better open your eyes,
If you want to find out,
'Cause I'm the she,
You been dreamin' about!"

The spotlight on Kaira kept changing colors and her **fringed outfit** seemed to **shimmer** and change with each new color.

"You been warned of her power,
*You been warned of her **charm**.*
They say when she loves you,
She causes bodily harm!

"Well, come a little closer,
If you want to find out,
'Cause I'm the she
They warned you about!"

If the people in the audience could have come any closer they would not have **hesitated**. The place was going crazy. Ginny shouted something into Armpit's ear, but he couldn't hear her. It didn't matter. He could feel her excitement.

When the song ended they both stood up and wildly applauded. Kaira looked over at them and smiled.

As the concert went on, the songs changed from fast to slow, from **funky** to **sincere**, but Kaira **maintain**ed a magical hold over the crowd. Even she could feel it. **Normal**ly she shut out the audience as she disappeared into the songs, but it was different tonight. It was almost like the audience was part of the band. She **fed off** their energy.

"I listen to the radio," she said. "So much of what I hear is filled with anger and **hatred**. It's like guys think they have to be tough and **cruel** in order to be a man. To me, a man is someone who is brave enough to love, and to let himself be loved."

Cotton, on drums, **pound**ed out a driving, steady beat, and Kaira **rip**ped **into** the next song.

"Angry Young Man, with your!
Angry Young Heart, and your!
Angry Young Eyes, and your!"

The drum **punctuate**d each line and **drove** it **home**.

"Angry young mouth, [BANG!] ***spewing***
Twist*ed cruel words. [BANG!] 'bout the . . .*
People you know, [BANG!] and the!

Money you make, [BANG!] and the!
Women you hurt, [BANG!] with your!
***Hateful** love."*

Armpit had heard the song before, but never with such **fire** behind it. Now, watching her, hearing her, seeing the passion in her eyes, it almost made him cry. The song could have been about him a couple of years ago, before he went to Camp Green Lake. Although it wasn't really Camp Green Lake that **releas**ed him from his anger. It was coming home and meeting Ginny.

"You'll be a Sorry old man, with a!
Sorry old heart, and two!
Sorry old eyes, with your!
*Sorry old **rage**, in your*
*Sorry old **cage** . . . ."*

She followed that with "**Imperfection**," and he was reminded of Tatiana. He had forgotten all about her. He was glad he'd **end**ed **up** going with Ginny instead, and it wasn't just because he got to be up **onstage**. Just seeing the look on Ginny's face as she stared at Kaira made him very happy.

Kaira started in on "**Damsel** in **Distress**," and Armpit grabbed Ginny's arm and told her to listen to the words, but it was hard to pick them out. The music was too loud, the audience was screaming, and the backup singers were singing some kind of counterpoint* harmony that kept getting in the way.

". . . these jewels, these shoes, this dress
A perfect picture of success.
No one would ever guess, Armpit,
A damsel in distress."

"Did you hear that?" he asked her.

She didn't know what he was talking about.

Of course she didn't. He knew that. He knew he had to be hearing something wrong.

Finally, at the very end of the song everything slowed down. The music got real soft, and the backup singers were silent, and even the audience was **hush**ed. Kaira, under a single spotlight, seemed especially alone and **vulnerable** as she half sang, half whispered the very last words.

"Save me, Armpit.
A damsel in distress."

At least, that was what he heard.

"So?" Armpit asked Ginny as they both stood and applauded.

"I like that song," said Ginny.

Kaira followed that with the fast-**paced** "Frying Pan," during which the words seemed to just shoot out of her mouth

---

★ **counterpoint** 대위법. 하나의 음표에 다른 음표를 덧붙이는 작곡 기술로, 화음을 만들 때 사용한다.

like **bullets**.

> *"An overworked, underloved, housewife named*
> *Myra*
> *Has dinner in the skillet,★ and a load in the dryer.*
> *When a magazine salesman comes to* ***inquire***
> *If she would like to be a magazine buyer,*
> *One look in his eyes, and she's filled with* ***desire.***
> *She buys a* ***subscription*** *to Time,✱ and one to*
> *Esquire.✱*
> *'Is there anything else, ma'am, that you require?'*
> *She says, 'Take me out of the frying pan . . .*
> *And into the fire!'"*

Armpit was amazed Kaira could get all the words out. There were three more **verses**, and each seemed to be faster than the one before it.

"Whew!" Kaira exclaimed when the song ended, and the audience laughed and applauded.

"Golly,❋" Kaira said. "So many of these songs seem to be about sex!"

This was greeted by **hoots** and more applause.

"You'd never guess I'm a **virgin**."

The crowd went wild over that, and the guitar player made a

★ **skillet** (= frying pan) 긴 손잡이가 달린 팬.
✱ **Time, Esquire** 미국의 잡지명.
❋ **golly** 어머나, 저런.

noise that sounded like he **pop**ped a **string**.

Every part of the concert was carefully planned and **script**ed, but Kaira had never said that before. The words just came out of her mouth. For once, she was having fun. She turned and waved to Ginny and her friend. Ginny waved back, but her friend looked **stun**ned, like a deer in headlights.

The band **launch**ed into the next song.

> *"I'm gonna take you for a ride,*
> *And we're gonna have some fun!*
> *I'm gonna take . . ."*

Armpit and Ginny turned and looked at each other. This had become their song. They **rose to their feet** and remained standing throughout the song.

"Whoo!" Armpit shouted.

Ginny laughed at him.

He held her hand as she **twirl**ed in a circle.

> *"I ain't never been* ***accused*** *of goin' too slow,*
> *So hang on, baby, and don't let go!*
>
> *"Oh, I got no* ***rearview mirror****,*
> *And none on either side.*
> *Got no rearview mirror,*
> *And none on either side.*
> *Ain't no lookin' back, babe,*

When I take you for a ride!"

When the song was over, Kaira **announce**d that she'd like to introduce a couple of friends of hers. To Armpit's **horror**, she turned to him and Ginny. He had a hard enough time just standing in the front of the room in speech class.

"Come on out," she said, **wiggling** her finger at them.

Ginny stood up, but Armpit remained **glue**d to his chair.

"You better go," said Terry, the soundboard operator, "or it will just get worse."

Armpit held Ginny's hand as they walked across the stage, but it was hard to say who was helping whom this time.

"These are my friends, Ginny, and . . ." Armpit thought she'd forgotten his name again, but she remembered at the last second.

". . . Theodore. They almost didn't get to see the show tonight. Some **low-life** ticket **scalper** sold them **counterfeit** tickets."

Everyone **boo**ed.

"Well, I guess you ended up with pretty good seats after all, didn't you?"

She held the microphone in front of Ginny.

"Yes," Ginny said, then **flinch**ed, **startle**d either by the sound of her **amplified** voice or by the **cheer**s of the audience.

"So how do you like the show so far?" Kaira asked her.

"It's awesome!" said Ginny, and everyone cheered in agreement.

"How about you?" Kaira asked, holding the microphone in front of Armpit.

He didn't know what to say. "Awesome," he **echo**ed.

No one cheered this time.

"I think it's awesome too," said Kaira. "In fact, I think it's the best damn show I've ever done!"

Cotton **rat-a-tat**ted on the drums in agreement.

"So, Ginny, what's your favorite song?"

Ginny didn't hesitate. "'Red Alert!'"

"You heard the lady!" The lead guitar **whine**d like a **siren** as the house **rock**ed with Kaira's biggest hit.

> *"I hear a w-w-warning sound*
> *Every time you c-c-come around . . ."*

She was dancing around Armpit and Ginny as she sang, and kept looking at Armpit as if he was the one she was singing about.

> *"Should you ch-chance to glance at me,*
> ***Threatens** my security."*

He didn't know what he was supposed to do.

Ginny was shouting "Red Alert!" right along with the backup singers, although he could only read her lips.

> *"Heart's a-th-**thumpin**'!*

Red Alert!
*N-n-**nerves** a-j-j-jumpin'!*
Red Alert!
All I hear is a s-s-siren sound."

At last Armpit managed to **ease** his way back to the safety of the soundboard, taking Ginny with him.

*"All systems are sh-**shutting** . . .*
*D-d-d-**down**!"*

Kaira shouted, "Thank you very much! I love you!" and she and the band left the stage.

The crowd shouted for more, Ginny and Armpit right along with them. The lights remained dark.

After about five minutes they came back out and did "Just Hold On a Little Longer." On the last line, "*. . . And then I'll be on my way,*" Kaira blew a kiss to the crowd and once again left the stage.

People continued to shout for more, but this time the **house lights** came on.

"Good show, Kaira," said Duncan.

Kaira was amazed. He had never said that to her before. None of the band members had. But something special had happened tonight; they could all feel it.

"What do you say we go back out and do one more?" said

Tim B.

"Sounds good to me," said Cotton.

Usually once the band was done, they were done. It was a job to them, nothing more. They did the one planned **encore**, and that was it.

"We've played all the songs we know," Duncan pointed out.

"Then let's play one we don't know," said Billy Goat.

Kaira laughed.

"Sounds good to me," said Cotton. "Any ideas, Kaira?"

"You want to try 'Piece of My Heart'?" Kaira suggested. She had been listening to the Janis Joplin CD and it was her favorite song.

"Let's do it," said Tim B.

The place went crazy when they stepped back out onstage.

"We've played every song we know," Kaira told the **raucous** crowd. "So now we're going to play one we don't know!"

It just might have been the worst **performance** ever of that song. Kaira had thought she knew the words, but she kept **skip**ping around to different parts of the song and repeating parts she'd already done as the band **struggle**d to **keep up** with her.

But nobody cared. It was pure fun, and the audience was having fun right along with them. It was the way rock 'n' roll was meant to be.

Even the cutesy-dootsy backup singers, two of whom had already changed back into jeans, came out, and were screaming

at the top of their lungs.

"TAKE IT!"
"Take another little piece
of my heart now, baby . . ."

The band tried to **improvise** a big finish, but in the end, the song just **fizzled** out.

"God, that was awful!" Kaira said with a laugh **amid** the thunder of applause, and then she and the band left the stage **for good.**

17

As an **army** of workers cleared the stage, **unhooking** power **cords**, removing **instruments** and **equipment**, Armpit and Ginny were unsure of what they were supposed to do or where they were supposed to go. When they stood up their chairs were taken away. They made sure to hold on to their souvenir cups.

There was no way down except through backstage. Besides, they had to get their regular shirts back from whoever had them. So, holding on to each other, they headed back through the curtain.

It wasn't as crowded as earlier, but the people who were there were in **constant motion**. Someone shouted, "Watch your back!" as a cart full of electronic equipment was **wheeled** past and out to a **loading dock**.

"Ginny!"

It was David, the red-**bearded** guy wearing the vest and no shirt. "Kaira's looking for you. Here, follow me."

Armpit followed too, and David didn't tell him not to. He led them along a very narrow **passageway**. As they turned the corner they saw and heard Kaira **arguing** with a large, **athletic**-looking black man, while Kaira's bodyguard stood off to the side.

". . . *could have* been your best **performance**," the man was saying, "but you know what the **critics** are going to write? 'She's no Janis Joplin.' All they're going to talk about is how you **butcher**ed her classic song!"

"We were having fun! Rock 'n' roll is supposed to be **spontaneous**!"

"Where'd you hear that?"

"Cotton."

"Cotton," the man repeated. He **glance**d at Armpit and Ginny. "This area is **off limits**," he said.

"They're my friends!" said Kaira. "I invited them."

The man **scowl**ed, then turned and walked away.

"Sorry about that," Kaira said. "So, you guys want some ice cream?"

"Yes," said Ginny.

"Uh, what **flavor**?" asked Armpit. He didn't know why he said that. Sometimes words seemed to come out of his mouth on their own.

"I'll check," Kaira said. She opened the door to her dressing room and went inside.

Armpit and Ginny remained in the hall.

"Well, come in," Kaira said to them, as if she thought they

were being stupid.

Ginny entered, followed by Armpit.

Kaira's bodyguard started to come in as well, but Kaira told him to wait outside.

Armpit was surprised by how small the room was—not much bigger than a **utility closet**. A small **couch** had been **squeezed** in between two walls, and a **miniature** refrigerator sat on the floor across from it.

Kaira opened the tiny refrigerator, and the even tinier **freezer compartment**, which was just big enough to hold a quart★ of ice cream. "It's chocolate chip," she told Armpit. "Is that okay?"

"Sure, fine," Armpit said, wishing he had never asked about the flavor.

"I can ask David to get you something else."

"Chocolate chip is my favorite ice cream!" he said, trying to put an end to the subject but instead sounding like a little kid.

Kaira **scoop**ed the ice cream into two plastic bowls and gave them each one. "Well, sit down."

"You should get the couch," said Armpit. "You're the star."

"Shut up," said Kaira.

Ginny laughed. "She told you to shut up."

"I know. I heard her."

Armpit sat on the couch next to Ginny. Kaira sat on the floor and ate her ice cream right out of the **carton**.

★ **quart** 액량의 단위 쿼트. 1쿼트는 약 1리터이다.

"I always get so hungry after a show," she said. "Before the show I'm too nervous to eat."

"You didn't seem nervous," said Armpit. "You seemed really cool."

Kaira laughed. "Cool? Look at me. I'm **drench**ed in **sweat**. It's **gross**!"

If Armpit knew her better he might have said, *You think you're **sweaty**. Man, you don't know what sweat is!* But he didn't **dare** say that to Kaira DeLeon.

"Why was that man y-yelling at you?" Ginny asked.

"Him? That's El—my manager," Kaira said. "He's all **piss**ed **off** 'cause of the last song. Oh, sorry, Ginny."

"It's okay," said Ginny. "I h-hear b-bad words at school."

"I thought that last song was great!" Armpit said.

"Well, I don't know about that," said Kaira.

"Is it a new one?" Armpit asked her.

"You never heard it before?"

"No."

"Don't tell me you've never heard of Janis Joplin?"

He hadn't, but he didn't dare **admit** it now. "Maybe I have," he said.

"If you'd heard her, you'd know. She's like my all-time favorite singer. You know, she was born right here in Texas."

"Have you met her?" asked Ginny.

"We're all going to meet Janis someday," said Kaira. "But it won't be in Texas." She turned back to Armpit. "Have you heard of the Beatles?"

"Shut up," he said.

Ginny **gasp**ed, but Kaira only laughed.

"So what grade are you in, Ginny?" Kaira asked.

"F-fourth. I was in fourth. I'm g-going into f-fifth."

"Fifth grade's great," said Kaira. "What about you? Are you still in school?"

"I'll sort of be a **senior** in high school."

"Oh, yeah? What sort of senior will you be?"

"He missed a year," Ginny explained. "He w-was at Camp Green Lake."

"She doesn't need to know about that," said Armpit.

"What's Camp Green Lake?"

"It's nothing," said Armpit.

"A **juvenile correct**ional **facility**," Ginny said, carefully **pronouncing** each word.

"You mean like a jail?" asked Kaira.

"It's a long story," Armpit said. "Four years ago I got in a fight and things got **out of hand**, and so I was sent to a kind of work camp for a year. And now I'm having to take summer school to try to **catch up**."

He wondered if Kaira now regretted shutting the door on her bodyguard.

"Can I tell her your nickname?" asked Ginny.

"No."

Kaira smiled. "What's his nickname?"

"Don't tell her, Ginny."

"Ginny?" **coax**ed Kaira.

"You better not," Armpit warned her.

"Come here, Ginny," said Kaira. "I want to tell you a secret."

Ginny slid off the couch, and Kaira **whisper**ed something in her ear. Then Ginny whispered something into Kaira's ear. They both looked at Armpit. Then Kaira whispered something to Ginny, and Ginny whispered something to Kaira.

Armpit didn't like it one bit. And he didn't like the way Kaira and Ginny smiled **conspiratorial**ly at each other either, when Ginny returned to the couch.

"You told her, didn't you?"

Ginny shook her head,

"She didn't tell me," Kaira said. She winked at Ginny. Ginny shut, then opened both eyes.

There was a knock at the door.

"Go away!" Kaira shouted.

The door opened anyway and a **bald**-headed black man entered. Armpit recognized the drummer.

"Oh, I didn't know it was you," Kaira said **apologetic**ally. "These are my friends, Ginny and Theodore. This is Cotton, our drummer."

"Well, not anymore," said Cotton. "Your dad just fired me. I just wanted to stop in and say good-bye."

"He can't do that!"

"He can, and he did."

"But I'm the one who wanted to sing that song!" Kaira said.

"Hey, don't worry. I'm cool with it. This really isn't the kind of music I should be making at this time in my life. I need to do something real."

"He's not my dad," Kaira said. "Just because he married my— As soon as I turn eighteen I'm firing his ass! Then I'll call you."

"You do that," Cotton said. "Nice to meet you," he said to Ginny and Armpit without looking at them, then left the dressing room.

"That **sucks**," Kaira said.

"Sorry," said Ginny.

"Yeah, me too," Kaira said. She sat in silence for a moment.

"Maybe we should go," Armpit said to Ginny.

"You know what I do all day?" Kaira asked. "I watch TV and play video games. All day."

That didn't sound too bad to him.

"I have no friends. But then finally, finally I find someone I can talk to. Someone I like. And so of course El Genius has to fire him. I **swear** that's the reason he was fired. Not because we did that song. Because he was someone I could talk to."

Armpit could only follow about half of what she was saying. "We really ought to get going," he said. "Ginny's mom will worry."

Kaira turned to Ginny. "You like your mom?" she asked.

"Yes."

"You're lucky," Kaira said. "How about you?" she asked Armpit.

"Yeah, I like Ginny's mom," said Armpit.

Kaira laughed. "You're funny. Man, you guys are so cool. It's so great you can be such good friends, when, you know, you're so different. I mean, different ages."

"Different colors, too," said Ginny.

Kaira went nose to nose with Ginny and said, "Well, *duh!*"

"*Duh!*" Ginny repeated, right back at her.

There was another knock on the door, and this time it was David with their shirts, washed, dried, and **neat**ly folded.

It was hard for Armpit to imagine this big, red-bearded guy washing their shirts.

Kaira gave Ginny a good-bye hug. Armpit wouldn't have minded one of those himself, but he just **shrug**ged and said, "Well, see ya."

"See ya," said Kaira.

"So what did you and Kaira whisper to each other?" he asked when they got back to the car.

"It's a secret," Ginny said.

"You're not going to tell me?"

"No."

"You're really not going to tell me?"

"No."

"After I take you to this concert and everything, you won't even tell me? Now I'm mad."

"Are you really mad?" asked Ginny.

"No."

"I didn't think you were."

"You didn't tell her my nickname, did you?"

"I j-just g-gave her a hint."

"A hint? What kind of a hint?"

"I said it was a p-part of the b-body."

"That's even worse!" He could just imagine what she was imagining. "Well, I guess it doesn't really matter," he said. "It's not like I'll ever see her again."

"Yes, you will," said Ginny.

"Oh, I will, will I?"

"Maybe."

18

"Do you realize it's after midnight?"

"That's how long concerts last."

"Then you should have left early."

"In the middle of the concert?"

"Yes! You had a **responsibility** to Ginny, and to her mother. You have no idea how worried she was! She was ready to call the police!"

Armpit knew that wasn't true. He had just come from Ginny's mother, who was **delight**ed that Ginny had had such a wonderful time.

"The best time of my whole life!" Ginny had said.

They had told her about having ice cream with Kaira DeLeon, but not about the counterfeit tickets. They just said that Ginny had gotten a little overexcited and **suffer**ed a **mild seizure**. She was taken to the medical **station**, where they met Kaira DeLeon, and so on.

Armpit didn't tell any of that to his own parents. He felt like he was under attack the second he walked in the door, and so didn't tell them anything except his name, rank, and serial number.★

He didn't have to work Sundays and would have slept late, but shortly after nine someone turned on his bedroom light. He **shield**ed his eyes as X-Ray smiled down on him.

"What are you doing here?" His voice was a little bit **hoarse** from the night before.

"Your mom let me in. Said it **serve**d you **right** for staying out so late."

When he and X-Ray were at Camp Green Lake together, they were **force**d to get up every morning at four-thirty. X-Ray always said that he'd sleep until noon every day once he was **release**d, but his **internal** clock was **permanent**ly **out of whack**. It had been more than two years since his release, and he still couldn't stay in bed past six-thirty.

"So I guess you got to see the concert," X-Ray said. "If you were out so late?"

The last bit of sleep slowly cleared from Armpit's brain, and the memory of the night before came back to him. "I'm going to kill you," he told X-Ray.

"Maybe your seats weren't quite as good, but at least you got

★ **name, rank, and serial number** 군인이 적군에게 잡히면 이름, 계급 및 일련번호를 말하는 상황을 이야기한다.

to see the show, right? No harm, no **foul**.★ Right?"

Armpit sat up and placed one foot on the floor. "First I'm going to put my pants on, and then I'm going to kill you."

The pants he'd worn the night before were on the floor of his room. "That's one leg," he said as he stepped into it.

"Wait, now just hold on a second. I got something here that just might **cool your jets**." X-Ray reached into his pocket and pulled out a **wad** of money. "Two hundred and ninety-eight dollars!"

"My pants are on," Armpit said, then slowly moved toward X-Ray, backing him against the wall.

"Look, I had to make a business decision," X-Ray said. "You weren't there, so I had to do what I thought was right."

Armpit **grab**bed him by the **collar**. "What you thought was *right?* You thought you were doing *the right thing*?"

"Look, what was I supposed to do? You kept calling me back, changing your mind. Sell the tickets. No, don't sell the tickets, I'm taking Tatiana. No, I'm not taking Tatiana. Sell 'em. No, don't sell 'em, I'm taking Ginny."

"And that's the last thing I said," said Armpit, shaking X-Ray on each word: "Don't . . . sell . . . the . . . tickets!"

"And I heard you," said X-Ray. "I heard you. But I already agreed to meet the **dude** at the H-E-B. That's the least I can do is still meet him, right? I can't **disrespect** him. So I get there,

---

★ **no harm, no foul** 어떤 규율이나 법을 위반했어도 실제로 해를 끼치지 않았다면 처벌할 필요가 없다는 말이다.

and I'm waiting in the parking lot, and I'm thinking, if only there was some way you and Ginny could go to the concert, and I could sell the tickets. And then suddenly, right in front of me is a big sign: *All Your Copying Needs*. I'm telling you, it was like a sign from God! I mean, how many times have I been to the H-E-B without noticing there was a Copy King right there? Did you know it was there?"

"God musta★ put it there just for you," said Armpit.

"So I go inside, but just to look around. Just to see what's *possible*, if you know what I'm saying. They had all different kinds of paper, and so I hold a ticket against the paper, **comparing**, you know, trying to find the right thickness. And then I made some copies—but just to see how they'd look, I swear! I wasn't planning to do anything with them.

"Then I got back outside, and the guy shows up, and I told him the tickets were no longer for sale. I did. I told him that. But he says he's **desperate**. He **offer**s me two hundred and fifty **apiece**. Sorry, I promised them to a friend. Three hundred? I mean, what am I supposed to do? I mean now we're talking a total of six hundred!"

Armpit **glare**d at him.

"You weren't there. I had to make a decision. Look, I thought you'd **figure out** what to do when you saw people in your seats."

"We got there first," said Armpit.

★ **musta** must have.

"That's impossible! I waited before coming to your house."

"So you just came over, handed me the tickets, without even a warning."

"I warned you. I told you to be **flexible**."

"Oh, I was flexible, all right. I had both arms **stretch**ed behind my back!"

"I was afraid you'd **blow** it," said X-Ray. "You're not a very good liar. You look all **guilty** and nervous and I was afraid you'd never make it past the ticket taker. But if you didn't know, you'd just **waltz** right in. I didn't want to disappoint Ginny."

Armpit grabbed him by the neck and lifted him off the floor.

The door to his room opened. He let go of X-Ray and backed away as his mother entered.

"You have a phone call."

"Uh, thanks." He took the phone from her, and she walked out. He hoped she hadn't seen the money on the bed.

"Hello?"

"Hi. I hope it's not too early."

"Uh, no, I just got up."

"We don't have to leave for Dallas until one. You want to get together and have breakfast or something?"

"Sure, that would be great."

"Cool! I'm staying at the Four Seasons. It's next to a river or lake or something. If you want I can look up the address."

"No, I know where it is," said Armpit. He had seen it from

the bus.

"Oh, and when you come, don't ask for Kaira DeLeon. You have to ask for Samantha Stevens."

"Is that your real name?"

"Yeah, I'm a **witch**." She laughed. "No, I always check in under a **fake** name. Have you ever watched that old TV show *Bewitched?*★"

"Is that the one with the genie?✱"

"No, dummy,❋ the one with the witch! It's not called *Begenied!*∗"

Armpit told her he'd be there in forty-five minutes. He had to shower first.

He **hung up**, then walked over to the bed and **scoop**ed up the money. "Two hundred and ninety-eight dollars?"

"It cost four dollars to make the copies. I **figure**d we'd **split** it."

Armpit stared at him.

"Okay, fine," said X-Ray. He **toss**ed in another two **bucks**. "So who was that?"

"Kaira DeLeon. Can you give me a ride to the Four Seasons? I'm supposed to meet her for breakfast."

★ **Bewitched** 미국 ABC 방송국에서 방영한 시트콤. 한 마녀가 인간과 결혼하여 전형적인 주부의 삶을 살아가는 내용이다.

✱ **genie** 알라딘의 요술램프에서 나오는 요정, 지니.

❋ **dummy** (속어) 바보, 얼간이.

∗ **Begenied** 주인공이 마녀가 아니라 지니일 경우 그 제목이 Begenied가 되어야 한다는 농담이다.

19

X-Ray's car was parked out front facing the wrong way. He opened the only door that worked, then slid over to the driver's side. "So really, where are we going?" he asked as Armpit got in beside him.

"The Four Seasons."

"Right, because Kaira DeLeon wants to have breakfast with you."

"Yes," said Armpit.

He didn't tell him anything more. It was his **payback** for the **phony** tickets.

The whole way there, X-Ray kept glancing sideways at him, trying to see a hint of a smile, or some kind of **clue**, but Armpit remained cool, as if nothing was out of the **ordinary**.

The X-Mobile turned off Cesar Chavez Avenue and into the hotel's **circular** driveway. A doorman opened Armpit's door for him.

"Excuse me," X-Ray said to him. "Is Kaira DeLeon staying here?"

"I wouldn't know, sir."

"Yes, you would. She's not here. You'd know if she was here."

Armpit thanked X-Ray for the ride, then walked through the **revolving** door into the hotel.

The inside of the hotel **remind**ed Armpit of pictures he'd seen of **ancient** Greek **temple**s, with stone **pillar**s and **marble** floors. He had no idea where he was supposed to go. The **concierge** seemed too **intimidating**, so he asked one of the **bellhop**s, who directed him to the house phone.★

Armpit picked up the receiver and **dial**ed zero.

"How may I direct your call?" the **operator** asked him.

He hung up.

He'd forgotten the name she'd given him. It was the lady from *Bewitched*, he knew that, but he couldn't remember her name. He could picture her perfectly, and could even hear the musical **note**s they played whenever she **twitch**ed her nose. Mary? Mindy? He was pretty sure it started with an "M."

A family of four came out of the elevator and headed in his direction. They all had **blond** hair. The husband could have been a tennis pro, and the wife looked like a model. The girls were **twin**s, about seven or eight years old.

★ **house phone** 내선 전화.

"Excuse me," Armpit said. "You ever watch the show *Bewitched?*" He knew he must have sounded crazy.

The father crossed in front of his daughters to **protect** them. He would have kept on going, hurrying his family along, but the mother stopped.

"What about it?" she asked.

"Do you remember the name of the woman, you know, the one who was the **witch**?"

She tried to remember. They all did.

"Elizabeth Montgomery," said the father.

"That doesn't sound right," said Armpit.

"I'm sure," said the father.

"That's the name of the actress," Armpit realized. "I need the name of the person on the show. You know, the name of the character."

"Oh, I thought you wanted the name of the actress," the father said, disappointed not to have been given the **credit** he thought he deserved.

"Her husband's name was Darren," said the wife.

"Samantha," said one of the girls.

"That's right!" said her mother. "Darren called her Sam, but her name was Samantha. Very good, Ashley."

"Do you remember her last name, Ashley?" Armpit asked the girl.

"Stevens," the father **declared** proudly. "Samantha Stevens."

"Thanks." Armpit picked up the phone and asked the operator for Samantha Stevens.

The blond family stared at him. "Is she staying at this hotel?" asked the father.

Five minutes later Kaira DeLeon stepped off the elevator, along with Fred, her bodyguard. Kaira wore **denim** shorts and a **sleeve**less top that stopped above her **belly button**. Her yellow toenails matched her flip-flops.★

"How ya doin', **Knuckles**?" she greeted him.

"Hi," he said.

"Was that it?" she asked. "Is Knuckles your name?"

"No, I didn't even get what you said."

"Is it Elbow?"

"I'm not going to tell you even if you guess it."

"It's Elbow."

"It's not Elbow."

Despite the weather, Fred was wearing a **tan** sports coat over a black T-shirt. He looked very stylish. If Armpit didn't know better, he would have guessed that he was the rich and famous one of the two.

"You hungry?" Kaira asked.

"**Starving**!" he said, and he had been, until he saw her. Now he was too nervous.

"The café here is really good."

She led the way down a **flight** of stairs. The hotel had been built on the side of a hill, so even though they went down,

---

★ **flip-flops** 엄지발가락과 둘째 발가락 사이에 끈을 끼워서 신는 샌들.

the café was still on ground level,* with an outdoor **patio** **overlook**ing the river.

"Three?" asked the **hostess**.

"Two," said Kaira. "And we don't want to sit too close to him either."

On the way to their table they passed the blond family seated at a **booth**. All four smiled and waved to Armpit like they were old friends. He waved back.

"You know them?" asked Kaira, more than a little surprised.

"Sort of."

They were seated at a table in the corner. Fred's table was far enough away to give them **privacy** but close enough for him to come to her **aid**, **just in case**.

A waiter came by with coffee and fresh-**squeez**ed orange juice. Kaira had coffee but no juice. Armpit had just the **opposite**.

"Muscles?" said Kaira.

"I'm not going to tell you either way."

She **dump**ed a **packet** of sugar into her coffee, then another one, and then a third.

"So you like sugar in your coffee," he said.

He felt **awkward**. They both did.

He was glad when the waitress brought them their menus so he had something to focus on. And when he saw the prices he was glad X-Ray had brought over the three hundred dollars.

---

* ground level 1층.

There was nothing on the menu for less than twenty dollars, and that included cereal.

"Toenail?" asked Kaira.

He didn't answer.

The waitress returned. Kaira ordered lemon ricotta★ pancakes, and he ordered corned-beef✱ hash❋ and eggs.

"How'd you get my phone number?" he asked her.

"David got it for me, from **security**."

"David," said Armpit. "He was the guy with the vest."

"What?"

"He wore a vest and no shirt."

"I didn't notice," said Kaira. "So what was it like at that camp? Was it hard?"

"Yeah."

"What'd you do there?"

"Dug holes."

"That all?"

"Pretty much. Every day another hole."

Kaira **nod**ded as if she understood, but he knew she didn't.

"You like being a famous singer?" he asked her. It was a stupid question, and he wished he hadn't asked it.

"It's all right," she said.

They sat in silence for a moment. It had been a lot easier to talk to each other when Ginny was there.

★ **ricotta** 리코타. 소젖 또는 양젖을 원료로 하는 부드러운 치즈.

✱ **corned-beef** 소금절인 쇠고기. 일반적으로 통조림 형태로 만든 것을 말한다.

❋ **hash** 작게 다진 고기와 감자를 섞어 튀긴 요리.

"Have you seen the **view** from the patio?" she asked him.

"No."

"You need to see the view," she said, in a voice that seemed **unusual**ly loud. "You can see the lake."

"It's actually a river," he said.

"Whatever," said Kaira.

"There's a huge **colony** of bats living under a bridge right by here," he told her.

"Bats?" Kaira said, again in an unusually loud voice. "Let's go look at the bats."

"You're not going to be able to see them now," Armpit said, but she was already out of her seat. "They only come out at night."

"We'll just look from the patio," Kaira said again rather loudly.

She was talking to him, but he got the feeling that everything she said was for Fred's **benefit**.

He followed her through the sliding glass doors★ out to the patio. A well-**manicured** **lawn** gently **slope**d away from the patio and down to a walkway. On the other side of the walkway the hill got much **steep**er and led down to the river.

"Nice view," he said.

Kaira took off her flip-flops. "Do you want to play **ditch** the **Doofus**?"

"What?"

★ **sliding door** 미닫이문.

She stepped off the patio and raced across the lawn.

For a second he was afraid he was the doofus, but then he remembered that was what she called her bodyguard. He watched her leap over the concrete walkway and disappear down the hill.

He took off after her but lost control as he headed down the steepest part of the slope. "Look out!" he shouted at Kaira, who was now standing on a **dirt** path beside the river.

As he tried to put on the **brakes**, she grabbed hold of his arm, and together they **spun** around three hundred and sixty degrees.

Kaira's face **bounced** hard against his shoulder.

"You all right?"

She laughed.

"That was close," Armpit said.

Kaira smiled at him as she let her **palm** slide down his arm, then held his hand.

They walked along the dirt path, continuing to hold hands. "So you're not worried I'll try to kill you now that you ditched your bodyguard?"

"You?" asked Kaira. "Are you **kid**ding? You're such a **wimp**."

Armpit **point**ed **out** the bridge with the bats.

"I don't like bats," said Kaira. "They're **creepy**."

"So, like has Fred ever had to save your life or anything?" he asked her.

"All you talk about is the Doofus!"

"I was just **curious**."

"Mostly he just keeps people from getting too close to me. Of course, it kind of makes it hard to meet guys. I mean, what guy wants to go out with a girl and her bodyguard? You try to kiss her and you **risk** getting your head **blown** off."

Did she squeeze his hand when she said the word "kiss"? If she did, it wasn't a big squeeze. Just a little **twinge**.

What he should have said was "I'll risk it," and then kissed her. That would have been really **smooth**, but by the time he thought of it, it was too late. The timing was off.

They continued along the river.

"I get all kinds of **weird** letters," said Kaira. "I've gotten seven marriage **proposals**! One guy **claims** to be a **billionaire** Arab prince."

"You think he really is?"

"Why, you want to marry him?" asked Kaira.

Armpit laughed.

"They're all freakazoids.★ There's this one who calls himself Billy Boy,✲ you know, like that song." She sang very softly: "*Oh, where have you been, Billy Boy, Billy Boy? Oh, where have you been, **charming** Billy?*"

Hearing her voice while holding her hand was almost too much for him to take.

"He wants to marry you?" asked Armpit.

"No, he wants to kill me."

"Really?"

★ **Freakazoid** 스티븐 스필버그가 제작한 TV 애니메이션. 여기에서는 'freak(괴짜)' 같은 의미로 쓰였다.

✲ **Billy Boy** 미국의 전래동요이자 자장가.

"Seriously. He's written like five letters so far, saying he's going to break my pretty little neck. I even got one at this hotel."

Armpit couldn't help looking around behind him.

Kaira laughed. "It's so **lame**," she said. "He even cuts out little letters and **glue**s them to the paper."

"You're not scared?"

"You'll protect me."

"Me? I'm a wimp."

"So tell me about you," said Kaira. "What are your big dreams? I mean, besides wanting to marry an Arab prince?"

"I don't have big dreams," Armpit said. "I just take small steps."

He told her about the advice the **counsel**or at the halfway house had given to him. The important thing was to take small steps and just keep on moving forward. "Life is like crossing a river. If you try to take too big a step, the **current** will **knock** you **off** your feet and carry you away."

"That's kind of **poetic**," said Kaira.

"I didn't make it up," said Armpit.

"My manager tells me I need to take big steps," she said. "I have to grab for everything I can get right now, because in a few years I could be all **wash**ed **up**."

"I doubt that," said Armpit.

"There's this song I'm writing." She sang again: "*Britney Spears is old and gray—she turned twenty-five today.* That's really all I've got so far."

"You write your own songs?"

"A couple. I wrote 'Angry Young Man' and '**Damsel** in **Distress**.' "

For a brief second he thought about asking her the words to "Damsel in Distress" but then thought better of it. It could only lead to his **embarrass**ment.

"And then El Genius—that's what my manager calls himself, El Genius—he had people kind of fix them up and **arrange** the music. He's such a control **freak**. Sometimes I think he's the one who's sending me the Billy Boy letters, just so he can have even more control over me. It's an excuse for having the Doofus watch me all the time. He's also married to my mother."

"Your bodyguard?"

"No, my manager. But I **bet** he just married her to have more control over me, because he's got a girlfriend, too. It doesn't matter. I'm going to **fire** him when I turn eighteen."

Armpit could only shake his head in wonder. She lived in such a different world.

"You've got nice strong hands," said Kaira.

"They're all **calloused** from digging."

"Is that your name? Hands?"

"No."

"Fingers? Are you the middle finger?"

Armpit dropped her hand. "I'll tell you what. I'll make you a deal. I'll tell you my name, but on one **condition**."

"What?"

"Whatever my name is, you have to touch me there."

Kaira took a step backward. "I have to touch you there."

"That's the deal."

She slowly looked him over, starting at his feet and working her way upward. "Ginny said it wasn't anyplace **nasty**."

Armpit **shrug**ged.

"You are so **mean**."

"Do you want to know or don't you?"

"Okay, tell me."

"Do we have a deal?"

"Yes, we have a deal."

Armpit waited a long moment, then quietly said, "Armpit."

Kaira **shriek**ed, causing several other walkers to turn and look at them.

"You are so bad," Kaira said. "Oh, you are so bad. Okay, raise up your elbow."

He did so.

She slowly moved her finger up the sleeve of his T-shirt, but he suddenly laughed and **pull**ed **away**.

"You're **ticklish**!"

She tried again, but again he couldn't stay **still**.

"Are you going to let me do this or not? Close your eyes."

He did so and waited. She held on to his shoulder. It was hard to keep still.

She quickly **poke**d her finger up his sleeve and **fulfill**ed her part of the **bargain**.

He opened his eyes.

"**Yuck**, it's all **sweaty**," she said as she wiped her finger on her shorts.

He started to explain about the **scorpion** but she wasn't interested. Her hand was still on his left shoulder, and now she placed her other hand on the right one.

He gently held her waist and felt her rise to her **tiptoe**s. He could feel blood **pulsating** against the tips of his fingers but couldn't tell if it was his or hers.

He **lean**ed toward her.

"What are you doing?" she **exclaim**ed, suddenly backing away.

"My job, Miss DeLeon," said a voice behind him.

20

"So you d-didn't kiss her?"

"I couldn't. Not with her bodyguard right there."

"I would have kissed her," said Ginny.

"*You* would have kissed her?" Armpit **tease**d.

Ginny **giggle**d at that. "I m-mean if I was you. If I was a b-b-boy."

Armpit ate a **spoonful** of Cheerios.★ They were in her half of the house. They were her Cheerios.

He knew Ginny was right. How many chances in your life do you get to kiss someone like Kaira DeLeon? He'd thought about nothing else since the moment Fred showed up.

Fred had **ruin**ed the moment, but as the three of them headed back to the hotel, Armpit had had it all planned out. Just before saying good-bye, he would say something **smooth**

★ **Cheerio** [상표명] O자 모양의 시리얼.

like "Next time you're in town, give me a call," and then kiss her.

But it never happened. Kaira's manager was in the hotel lobby when she returned, and she started **yell**ing at him for firing the drummer, and he told her that drummers were **a dime a dozen**. Kaira was **practically** in tears. She told Armpit she was "sorry about all this," then went **sulk**ing off into the elevator.

"She told me to say hi to you."

"She did?"

"Yeah. She thinks you're really cool."

Ginny smiled. Her glasses slid down her nose and she pushed them back in place.

"What happened to the f-food?"

"What food?"

"At the café."

Armpit laughed because he had wondered about that too. After Kaira went up in the elevator, he went back to the restaurant to check.

"They threw it away."

"Too bad," said Ginny.

"Yeah, I woulda liked to have tried those twenty-nine-dollar eggs."

"Did you have to pay for them?"

"No, everything was **charge**d to her room, but it's not like she pays for it either. Everything's charged to the tour. It's a whole other world. It's no **big deal** to them to pay a hundred dollars for breakfast."

"No wonder t-tickets cost so much," said Ginny.

"You're right."

A car parked in front of their house and a young white woman got out. They watched her through the front window as she stepped onto the **porch**.

"You know her?" Armpit asked.

"No."

Skin color was usually a **reliable indicator** as to which half of the house a visitor was heading for, but this woman was the **exception** to the rule. She checked her small notebook, then knocked on Armpit's front door.

"Maybe Kaira sent her," said Ginny.

He had been hoping the same thing. He went to the door. "May I help you?"

The woman turned around. "I'm looking for Theodore Johnson."

"I'm Theodore."

The woman checked the address on the door.

"You're right. That's were I live," Armpit explained. "I'm just over here right now."

"Oh, then I guess you're Ginny McDonald."

"Yes," Ginny said, at Armpit's side.

The woman took a black wallet from her purse. "I'm **Detective** Debbie Newberg from the Austin Police **Department**." She opened the wallet, showing them her badge. "I wanted to talk to you about the concert tickets."

Armpit **struggled** to keep his **composure.** "You want to talk to both of us, or just me?" he asked.

"Were you with him when he bought the tickets?" she asked Ginny.

"No."

"Then just you, if you don't mind."

Armpit went out one door and in the other. He led Detective Newberg into the living room and **offer**ed her something to drink, but she **declined**. He sat at one end of the red and blue **plaid couch**, and she sat across from him on an ottoman,★ her knees close together and her notebook on her **lap**.

She seemed too young and too pretty to be a police officer. She had bright brown eyes, and curly black hair very similar to Kaira's. Her cheeks had a red **glow** to them, as if she was **blush**ing.

"So I understand you paid six hundred dollars for the tickets, is that **correct**?"

He hated to start right out with a lie, but it was the path of least **resist**ance. "Yes, ma'am."

"Was that six hundred total, or six hundred per ticket?"

"Total," he said. "Three hundred per ticket."

"That's a lot of money."

He suddenly felt very **conscious** of the old and well-**worn** furniture. Everything in his house seemed **shoddy** and cheap.

★ **ottoman** 좌석이 낮고 옆으로 긴, 등받이가 없는 의자.

"Well, I wasn't planning to pay that much," he said. "It was supposed to be only a hundred and thirty-five a ticket, but then the guy kept changing his mind. First they were for sale. Then they weren't. Then they were again. Three hundred's not really that much for Kaira DeLeon tickets. They went for seven hundred and fifty in Philadelphia."

"Wow," said Detective Newberg.

He tried to relax. He wasn't a **suspect**, he **remind**ed himself. He was the **victim**. She was here to help him.

"What do you mean they were only *supposed to cost* one hundred and thirty-five?"

"There was an **ad** in the paper."

The second he said that, he knew it was a mistake. She could easily **get ahold of** last week's newspapers and find the ad, along with X-Ray's phone number.

"What newspaper was that?" she asked.

"It wasn't really a newspaper. It was one of those free advertisements, you know, that they **stick** on your door."

"Do you still have it?"

"No, it got **recycled**."

"Do you remember what day it was placed on your door?"

"No. It might have been two weeks ago. I just don't remember."

"And the ad was for a hundred and thirty-five dollars?"

"No, I don't think it was that much."

"You just said—"

"It was for ninety-five," Armpit said **firm**ly. "But that was two weeks ago. By the time I called the guy, he said the price had gone up to a hundred and thirty-five so I told him I had to think about it. Then when I called him back on the day of the concert, he said the tickets were no longer for sale. But then he called me back and said they were for sale again, but the price was now two hundred. But then when I tried to buy the tickets he said they weren't for sale again."

"And that's when you offered him three hundred?"

Armpit nodded. "I was **desperate**. It was five-thirty. The concert was at eight. I'd already promised Ginny."

"Did he ever tell you his name?"

He shook his head.

"It wasn't in the ad?"

"No," said Armpit. "Look, why— I mean, what's the big deal? Ginny and I **ended up** getting to sit on the stage. You know—no harm, no **foul**?"

"Well, our **mayor** seems to think there was quite a bit of harm. She saw what happened to Ginny, and to you, and she wants to get the guy."

"What will happen to him?" Armpit asked, trying to sound only **mildly curious**. "Will he have to go to jail?"

"Oh, I doubt it. We're just talking six hundred dollars."

He tried not to let his **relief** show on his face.

"Unless he has a prior criminal record,★" said Detective Newberg.

★ **prior criminal record** 전과.

Armpit sat up straight.

"So your **initial** contact with him was by phone?"

It took Armpit a moment to **decipher** the question. "Um, yes."

"I don't suppose you remember his phone number?"

"No."

She smiled. Her cheeks turned pink. "I wouldn't expect you to. So then, where did you meet him?"

"At H-E-B. In the parking lot."

"And how did you **recognize** each other?"

"I didn't. I never saw him before in my life."

Detective Newberg raised her eyebrows. "What I'm asking is, how did you find each other in the parking lot? How did you know he was the one selling the tickets?"

"Oh." Armpit noticed his Raincreek cap **hang**ing on the back of the door. "I said I'd be wearing a red cap."

He got up and got the cap. It felt good to get up and move around.

He showed her the cap, but she didn't seem all that interested. He put the cap on his head. "So then he drove up beside me, and we **bargain**ed a little, like I said, and then I gave him the money, and he gave me the tickets." He sat back down on the arm of the couch. He removed the cap and set it on the cushion beside him.

"What kind of car was he driving?"

"A white Suburban."

"And where were you standing?"

"On the **curb**."

"In front of the H-E-B?"

"No, a few stores over. I think it was in front of Copy King."

Why did he say that? Sometimes it felt like the words just jumped out of his mouth. "Was he the only one in the car?"

"Yeah."

"So he was driving on the wrong side of the road."

"He was?"

"If the driver's side was next to the curb."

"Oh, yeah, I guess so," said Armpit. He realized he had to be more careful. "I didn't notice because there weren't any other cars around."

"At five-thirty?" asked Detective Newberg. "Man, I should start shopping there!" She smiled. "The H-E-B by me is **jam**med that time of day."

Armpit shrugged.

"So what did he look like?"

"I didn't get a real good look."

"You were face to face, weren't you, when he rolled down his window?"

"I was thinking about the tickets, not what he looked like."

"Was he white? Black? Hispanic?"

"Kind of black."

"Kind of black?"

"I think he might have been Iranian.★"

★ **Iranian** 이란인.

Iranian? Where did that come from?

"You think he was Iranian?"

"Maybe part black, part Iranian," Armpit said. "Now I remember. He said his name was Habib. That's why I think he's part Iranian."

Officer Newberg raised her eyebrows. "Habib?" She wrote the name in her little black notebook.

"Did he speak with an accent?"

"Um, yeah, kind of."

"An Iranian accent?"

"Yeah."

"Was he tall? Short? Thin? Fat?"

"Kind of big," Armpit said. "But it was hard to tell because he was sitting down in his car."

"How old?"

"Maybe about your age."

"How old do you think I am?"

He studied her face. "Twenty-three?"

"I'm twenty-eight." She smiled. "So we'll say he's in his twenties. Any **distinguish**ing **characteristics**?"

"No."

"**Tattoo**s? Facial hair?"

"Oh, yeah. He had a **mustache**."

"Nice of you to **mention** it."

"I didn't think it was important. I mean, he probably **shaved** it off by now, don't you think?"

She shrugged. "Anything else come to mind?"

He shook his head.

"You sure?"

"Not that I remember."

"Okay, well, this is a good start. I'm going to talk to some of the other people seated nearby at the concert. Maybe they also bought their tickets from Habib."

She gave him a card with her name and phone number on it and told him to call her if he remembered anything else.

He shook her hand. It felt cool and soft.

As he watched her drive away, he felt bad about having to lie to her. She was nice. She had a sweet smile. It was hard to imagine her out in the world, fighting criminals. He worried she might get hurt.

21

X-Ray **pace**d back and forth by his car, which was parked in front of Armpit's house. "We got nothing to worry about," he said. "Nothing to worry about. The police have better things to do than to **launch** a big **investigation** over a couple of **phony** tickets."

Armpit had told him everything, including how he had met Kaira.

"Man, I wish you had talked to me first," X-Ray said. "I could have **come up with** something believable."

"I think she believed me," said Armpit.

"*Habib?*" X-Ray shook his head. "And you never should have **mention**ed the H-E-B."

"Yeah, I wasn't thinking."

"Well, that's **obvious**. Look, if she **interrogate**s you again, just remember one word: 'kiss.' K-I-S-S. Keep It Simple, Stupid!"

"I think she believed me."

"You know we're in this together. We **split** the money, fifty-fifty."

Yes, he realized that.

"Not to worry," X-Ray said. "The **cops** have better things to do. Man, it's just my luck the mayor was at the concert! What kind of mayor goes to rock concerts?"

"You're lucky she was there," Armpit **pointed out**.

"Oh, yeah? How's that?"

"If the mayor wasn't there, I woulda been sent to jail, Ginny woulda been taken to a hospital and **had her stomach pumped**, and you'd be dead."

X-Ray laughed. "You're such a **joker**."

At school on Monday, Tatiana wanted to know all about the concert. "You still went, didn't you?"

"Oh, I had a great time. Too bad you missed it."

"Were you able to find someone to go with you?"

"Yeah, that wasn't a problem."

"A girl?"

He **nod**ded.

"Well, good. I'm really glad you had such a good time!"

"She wore this thing with long white **fringe**—"

"You know what?" said Tatiana. "I really don't care what your girlfriend was wearing."

"My girlfriend? No, you asked me to tell you what Kaira DeLeon had on."

"I don't have time for this now," Tatiana said, then walked

away.

In **economics** he gave Matt Kapok the dollar back.

Matt seemed surprised. "Uh, thanks, Arm—" His white face turned even whiter. "I mean, I mean, I mean, Theodore. Thanks, Theodore."

"You really helped me out," Armpit said. "I **owe** you one."

On the back of their **souvenir** T-shirts was a list of the fifty-four cities on the tour. Ginny and Armpit looked at them every day for the next week and a half and tried to **predict** where Kaira was.

"Maybe she'll call from Albuquerque,★" said Ginny, studying the T-shirt. "Al-bu-quer-que," she repeated. She liked saying that word.

Armpit laughed. "She's not going to call," he said, as if he never **gave** it **a thought**, when in truth it was **practically** all he'd thought about since he'd last seen her. Every time the phone rang his body went to red **alert**. He hated leaving the house for school or work because he was afraid he might miss her call. But after a week and a half, that didn't seem too likely anymore.

"It's like she says in her song," he told Ginny. "She'll **get around** to you, and then she'll be on her way."

He just wished he could have held on a little bit longer.

He had failed a quiz in economics earlier that day. He hadn't read the last two chapters. He couldn't **concentrate**.

★**Albuquerque** 앨버커키. 뉴멕시코주 중부에 있는 도시.

At work the day before he'd installed a **sprinkler** system in the front yard of a house. Jack Dunlevy had trusted him to do the **entire** job himself.

Armpit had made sure the sprinkler heads were **even**ly **distribute**d, so that the water would cover the entire **lawn**. He had carefully **secure**d each connection.

The problem was that it was all just **attach**ed to itself. The pipes formed one giant **rectangle**, with no way for any water to enter the system.

He ended up having to work overtime, digging a new **trench**, cutting into the pipes, and attaching the main water line. "You don't have to pay me for the extra time it took," he told his boss. "I'm the one who **screwed up**."

"Unfortunately, I do," said Jack Dunlevy. "It's the law."

How could he explain it was all because a Kaira DeLeon song came on the radio?

At least he hadn't heard from **Detective** Newberg again. Maybe X-Ray was right. The Austin Police Department had better things to do than investigate who had sold **counterfeit** tickets to an African American teenager who lived on the wrong side of I-35.

He wondered if she had checked his record and found out about his **prior conviction**. He didn't want her to think badly of him.

Cherry Lane called once, to ask how he was doing. His mother had answered the phone and was very **impress**ed when she realized who she was talking to.

Armpit was disappointed it wasn't Kaira.

"Why'd the mayor call you?" his mother asked him.

"Remember, I told you I met her? I did some work at her house."

For the first time in a long while, his mother looked at him and saw someone who maybe wasn't all bad.

Now it was Thursday evening, eleven days since he saw Kaira, and he was trying to **get through** a chapter in economics. The final exam was in eight days.

He'd thought about asking Matt Kapok if he might want to study together. They greeted each other every day in class. But he didn't want to leave the house, **just in case** Kaira called, and he would have been **embarrass**ed to invite Matt over here, where, who knows, his parents might **accuse** Matt of being a drug **dealer**.

The speech final was also a week from Friday, but he wasn't too worried about that. There were no more speeches **due**, and the **stuff** in the book was all obvious stuff, like how you should look your **prospective employer** in the eye at a job interview.

He reread a **paragraph** in his econ book and studied the graph next to it. It was just beginning to **make sense** when the phone rang, **shatter**ing his thoughts.

He waited nervously for a moment before returning to the graph.

"Theodore, telephone!" his mother called.

He tried to remain calm. Most likely it was just X-Ray. He

took a deep breath, then went into the kitchen.

His mother mouthed the words "a girl" as she handed him the phone.

"Yeah, hi," he said, trying to sound **casual**.

"Hi, how's it going?"

He recognized the slightly **nasal** voice of Detective Debbie Newberg. He walked back into his bedroom as he spoke to her.

"Oh, uh, fine."

"You probably thought I'd forgotten about you."

"Uh, no, not really."

"How certain are you that the guy's name was Habib?"

"Not real certain."

"Could it have been Felix?"

"Felix? No, I don't think so."

"How about Moses?"

"No. I'm pretty sure he said it was Habib."

"Maybe he had a nickname. Is that possible?"

"I guess."

"Did he ever refer to himself as X-Ray?"

He took a breath, then said he'd never heard that name before. "How about Armpit?"

He almost dropped the phone.

"Hello? Are you there?"

"Yeah. Yeah, I'm here."

"Does Armpit **ring a bell**?"

"No, I think I would have remembered a name like that."

Debbie Newberg laughed. "I suppose so," she said.

Armpit looked at his economics book opened on his desk. He knew he could forget about studying tonight.

22

A letter came the next day. Armpit checked the mail when he got home from school. It was addressed to Theodore A. Johnson, and its return address was the Hotel del Coronado in San Diego. His middle name was Thomas.

The letter was written with a purple pen on hotel **stationery** in **remarkably neat** handwriting.

Dear T (or should I say Dear A?),

I hope you don't mind a long and ***dopey*** *letter. I know it's going to be long and dopey, because every letter I've written to you has been long and dopey. They just keep getting longer and dopier! Of course, I don't actually mail them, so I guess it doesn't matter whether you mind or not.*

I always say all kinds of stupid things about how much I miss you, and wish you were here, and ***lame junk*** *like that. Once I even used the L word!* How* ***dumb*** *is that???*

Nobody falls in L after a bowl of ice cream and a ten-minute walk! Now you know why I didn't mail the letters. I may be dumb, but I'm not stupid!!!

It's just that you and Ginny are really my only friends. Is that ***pathetic*** *or what? I don't mean you and Ginny are pathetic. I'm the one who's pathetic!*

It feels good to write to you, even if I know you'll never read it. It sure ***beat****s talking to my* ***shrink****. I can see your face in my mind. Your eyes. Your smile makes me feel safe.*

I'm so mad Dr. Doofus showed up when he did. That's my new name for him. He's a doctor of doofology.✱

I think you were going to kiss me. I know I wanted you to kiss me. I still do. Oh, so much!

God, this is even worse than yesterday's letter! You know, I almost sent it to you. I put a stamp on it and everything. There was a mail ***slot*** *by the elevator. I held the letter over the slot. I'd lift one finger, then another. It was kind of like standing on the edge of a* ***cliff****, wondering what it would be like to jump.*

Do you think I'm ***insane****? Of course not, because you're not reading this.*

When I sing love songs, it helps for me to picture someone in my mind. I used to just make up some imaginary boy of my dreams and sing about him. He looked nothing like

---

★ **L word** L로 시작하는 단어 'love'를 말한다.

✱ **doofology** 'doofus(멍청이)'에 학문을 나타내는 접미사 'ology'를 더해서 '멍청이학'이라는 단어를 만들었다.

you. He was much more handsome. Just kidding. Anyway, now, when I sing those songs, I picture you.

Don't get all **freaked** *out. I'm not saying I love you. It just helps me sing the songs.*

I wonder what you'd think if you actually read this.

Okay, Kaira, this is getting scary. You're not going to mail this letter. You're not! You're not! No way!!!!

Okay, I'm going to have to write something really embarrassing now. Then I can be sure I'll never mail it.

Okay, here goes.

I liked it when I touched your armpit. It made me feel all **goosey** *inside.*

Aaaah!

Oh, I miss you so much!!!!

XOXOXOX★

Kaira

★ XOXOXOX 'hugs and kisses'의 약자로 편지의 마지막에 쓰는 문구.

23

"Wow," Armpit said, then read the letter again. He imagined her holding the **envelope** above a mail **slot**, closing her eyes, and letting it go. Maybe she screamed.

He wished he knew how to **get in touch** with her. He looked at the back of the T-shirt. She probably was in Los Angeles now, but he had no idea what hotel she was staying at, or what TV character's name she was using.

It was too bad she didn't include her cell phone number, but why would she? She never planned to mail the letter.

The phone rang.

He **grab**bed it before the second ring. "Hello?"

"Theodore, good, I'm glad you're home."

It was **Detective** Newberg.

"We've got a **suspect** down at the **station**. I'd like you to be here while I question him."

He didn't know what to say. "I have to go to work. I only

just got home from school."

"What time do you need to be there?"

"One o'clock. I don't even know the address of where I'm supposed to be."

"I can have an officer take you wherever you need to go."

"And I got to eat lunch first."

"What kind of pizza do you like?"

"*Pizza?* Uh, pepperoni."

"I'll send a **patrolman** to get you."

He **hung up** with Detective Newberg and called Raincreek. He got the address and left a message that he might be a little late, and that he wouldn't need Hernandez to give him a ride.

Less than ten minutes later a patrol car **pull**ed **into** the driveway.

"Can I sit in the front seat?" Armpit asked. "I don't want my neighbors to think I'm being **arrest**ed again."

He regretted those words as soon as they **escape**d his mouth, but the police officer just said, "Sure, **hop in**." Maybe the officer hadn't heard him exactly. Or else the cops already knew about his **criminal** record.

The police station was a three-**story** stucco★ building. Armpit **recognize**d the place. It was where he had been taken after the fight in the movie theater.

A sign warned that all visitors were **subject** to search, but he just walked through the metal **detector** and went with the officer

★ stucco 치장회반죽. 회반죽, 석고, 고운 모래를 섞어 만든 건축 재료.

up to the second floor.

Detective Newberg stepped out of a room, saw Armpit, and gave him a little wave. "Come have a look," she said, then put her finger to her lips, indicating for him to be quiet.

He went with her back into the room, which was dark and smelled like pizza. One slice had already been eaten from the box on the table.

"It's good pizza," said Debbie Newberg. Her cheeks reddened.

A window looked out into another room. The room was almost **identical** to his but brightly **lit**. X-Ray was sitting at a table, his fingers **drum**ming nervously. Armpit could hear the **tap**ping through the speakers on the wall.

"Is that Habib?" Detective Newberg asked quietly.

He almost laughed but then just shook his head.

"You're sure?"

"**Definite**ly not him."

"I want you to listen while I interview him, and let me know if anything he says **strikes a chord**."

She gave him a **pad** of paper and a pen out of her **briefcase** in case he wanted to make notes.

She left him alone in the room, then a moment later sat down across from X-Ray. Armpit listened while she advised X-Ray that even though he was not under arrest, he still had the right to remain silent, and the right to have an **attorney** present during questioning.

Armpit had never known X-Ray to remain silent.

"Why would I need a lawyer?" X-Ray asked. "I'm **cooperating**, right? Write that down. I'm being cooperative."

Detective Newberg **flash**ed her girlish **smile**, then made a note on her yellow pad.

Don't be fooled by her smile, Armpit thought, trying to **telepathic**ally send the message through the wall.

"You understand that you are not under arrest and are free to leave whenever you wish."

X-Ray **nod**ded.

"Please answer **audibly**."

"**Affirmative**," said X-Ray.

"You also understand that this interview is being recorded."

"Affirmative," X-Ray said again.

"You also understand that although you are not under arrest, you are still a suspect in this case. Anything you say today may later be used as **evidence** in **court**."

"Affirmative," said X-Ray. He liked saying that word.

"And that you have the right not to answer any questions, and you're **knowing**ly and freely giving up that right."

"Like I said, I want to cooperate. I got nothing to hide, right?"

"Will you state your name for the record?"

"Rex Alvin Washburn."

"And your age?"

"Seventeen."

"Do you ever go by a name other than Rex?"

"No."

"X-Ray, perhaps?" Again she smiled.

"X-Ray?" X-Ray repeated.

"Before you say something stupid, I think you should know I spoke to several people who bought concert tickets from someone who called himself X-Ray. His cell phone number is the same as yours. And we've seen the **license** plate on your car."

"Right, I was just about to tell you that. You have to give me a chance. You can't just ask questions without giving me a chance to explain."

"Sorry."

"See, when you asked if I had another name, I don't really think of X-Ray as another name. It's pig latin★ for Rex. See, like you're Debbie, right? So in pig latin that would be Ebbie-Day. It's the same name, just a different language."

"I understand," Detective Newberg **reassure**d him. "So just to be clear, when these people told me they bought tickets from X-Ray, they really bought them from you."

"Right. My point exactly."

"How many tickets did you sell?"

X-Ray **hesitate**d. Armpit knew what he was thinking. He was trying to **figure** what she knew, and if it was **worth** lying about.

"Twelve."

"You sure it wasn't fourteen?"

★ **pig latin** 피그 라틴. 은어를 만드는 방법 중 하나로, 단어의 맨 앞에 있는 자음을 맨 뒤로 보내고 거기에 ay를 덧붙이는 말장난이다. X-Ray라는 이름도 Rex에서 R을 ex(X) 뒤로 보낸 후 ay를 붙여서 나오게 된 이름이다.

"No, just twelve."

"How much did you sell them for?"

"I **charged** a small service fee. It's not **illegal**. It's called free **enterprise**, **protected** by the **Constitution**."

"How much?"

"I didn't **twist** anybody's arm. They all came to me. They wanted the tickets, and I charged a **fair** price. If they didn't think it was fair, they didn't have to buy them."

"I just want to know how much."

"A hundred and thirty-five dollars."

"Did you sell any for any more than that?"

"Yeah, I sold two for three hundred."

"Three hundred each ticket, or three hundred total?"

"Each. But I had **expenses**, too, you know. It wasn't all **profit**. I had to pay for an **ad** in the newspaper. And gasoline's not cheap. Plus I stood in line for like six hours. Time is money, right?"

"Did you have a partner?"

"No. I'm **independent**."

"Ever heard of someone named Habib?"

"Habib? No."

"How about Armpit?"

X-ray didn't even **flinch**. "Armpit? Is that really like someone's name?"

"**Apparently**. So you don't know him?"

X-Ray shook his head.

"Please answer audibly."

X-Ray **chuckle**d and said, "No, I never heard of nobody named Armpit."

"How did you first go about **acquiring** the tickets?"

"Say what?"

"The tickets you sold. Where did you get them? You **mention**ed standing in line for six hours."

"Right. I acquired them the day they went on sale."

"At the Lonestar **Arena**?"

"Right. I got there the night before and waited in line for like twelve hours."

"How much did you pay for the tickets?"

"Seven hundred and twenty dollars. Talk about a **rip-off**. They're supposed to sell for fifty-five a piece, but they charge a five-dollar service charge for each ticket."

"That doesn't seem fair," Detective Newberg agreed. "But here's something I don't get. I heard there was a limit of six tickets per customer. How did you manage to buy twelve?"

"I just did."

"I heard they were pretty **strict** about that."

"You're right. Okay. Here's what happened."

Keep It Simple, Stupid, thought Armpit.

"Like you said, you can only buy six tickets. Six tickets *at a time.* There's nothing that **prevent**s someone from buying six tickets, then getting back in line and buying six more tickets."

"But it was a long line, wasn't it?"

"Yeah, it was. But you can always pay someone like fifty dollars to cut in line. See, that's another expense. That's what

I'm talking about. People think ticket **scalpers** just make tons of money, but the expenses can really add up."

"That wasn't what I was thinking," said Detective Newberg. "You want to hear what I was thinking?"

"Go ahead."

"Thank you. I was thinking about the fact that all twelve tickets were in the same **row**, right next to each other. I'm wondering how you could buy six, then go back in line and buy six more, and they're all right next to each other."

"I can explain that."

"I suggest you don't," said Detective Newberg.

"But you said—"

"I don't want to hear your explanation," Detective Newberg said.

"See, I never said I went back in line. I said you *can* pay someone to cut in line, but I didn't say I—"

"Shut up and listen!"

X-Ray stopped talking.

"It's a **crime** to give **false** information to a police officer. And for someone like yourself, with a **prior offense** and still on **probation**, you could be facing quite a bit of jail time."

"You know about that?" asked X-Ray.

"You're not dealing with children here. Let me tell you what else I know. I know you went to a restaurant called Smokestack Lightnin' with somebody named Armpit. So I know you lied when you said you didn't know him. Any other lies you want to tell me?"

X-Ray didn't answer.

"You see that mirror? You're a smart guy, X-Ray. Do you think that's a regular mirror? You think it's in here so I can fix my **makeup**?"

"No," X-Ray answered quietly.

"No, it's a two-way mirror. Behind it is an **expert** criminal **psychologist**. He's watching and listening to everything you say. He knows when you're lying just by your body language, and by the **inflection** of your voice."

X-Ray gave a little wave to the "psychological expert."

Armpit waved back.

"So what I want you to do is think about everything you told me, and see if there are any **correct**ions you might want to make."

"See, if you just let me explain—"

"Think before you talk," said Detective Newberg. "And you better tell me the truth this time, or else the DA★ will get this recording."

"I'm tryin' to tell you the truth, if you'll just listen. You're right, I didn't buy all the tickets myself, but it was my money! Look, let's say you're at the store, and all you want to buy is a candy bar, but there's a real long line. And then you see somebody you know at the front of the line, so you give her your dollar and she buys the candy bar for you. Then later, if someone asks you where you got the candy bar, you'll say you

★ DA (= District Attorney) 미국의 지방 검사.

bought it at the store. It's not a lie, is it?"

"Who helped you buy the tickets?"

"Armpit."

"Do you know his real name?"

"Habib, I think."

"You think?"

"I don't know the **dude**! I **swear**! Felix called him Armpit. I never even saw the dude until that day in line. See, I went to buy my tickets, and they told me I could only buy six, like you said. So then Felix and Armpit show up, and Armpit **offer**s to buy the other six for me. Man, that was the biggest mistake I ever made in my life."

"How do you mean?"

"You know, I thought I would just have to pay Armpit fifty **buck**s or something, for doing that for me. But no. He **insist**ed I make him my partner. And let me tell you something else. Armpit is not someone you can say no to. I'm talking big, and mean, and tough. That's why I lied and said I didn't know him. If I'm going to have to **testify** against Armpit, then you better put me in the **witness** protection program.★"

"What was your **arrange**ment with him?"

"We **split** all the profits, fifty-fifty. He was there with me for every sale."

"Do you know his last name?"

★ **witness protection program** 증인 보호 프로그램. 증인이 피고에 대해 불리한 증언을 하여 위협을 받을 수 있는 경우, 그 증인을 보호해주는 프로그램이다.

"No."

"Where does he live?"

"I have no idea."

"Do you know his phone number?"

"No."

"I'm getting tired of this, Rex."

"I swear. I'm not lying!"

"Then how would you get in touch with him?"

"I'd call Felix. Then Felix would call Armpit, and we'd meet at H-E-B."

"Who kept the tickets?"

"He kept six, I kept six. To be honest, I thought he was going to **rip** me **off**, but he never did."

Detective Newberg set her briefcase on the table and un**latch**ed the **clasp**s.

"Look, I'm sorry for not being totally straight with you earlier," X-Ray said. "Armpit scares the bejesus★ out of me. But now I told you the truth, so everything's cool, right?" He smiled. "No harm, no **foul**?"

Detective Newberg suddenly turned and seemed to stare right at Armpit, although he knew she couldn't see him.

She looked away, then removed two photographs from her briefcase. "Is this Felix?"

"Yeah, that's him."

She showed X-Ray a photo of Moses. "Is this Armpit?"

★ **bejesus** [감탄사] 제기랄, 맙소사.

X-Ray took his time studying the photo. "No, Armpit's got dark skin. And he didn't wear a cowboy hat. He wore one of those things, what are they called, a turban? I think he might be part Iranian."

"Did he have a **mustache**?"

X-Ray thought a moment.

Armpit couldn't remember if he told X-Ray he'd said Habib had a mustache.

"He might have. The guy was so hairy it was kind of hard to tell. He's the kind of guy who has to **shave** three times a day, if you know what I mean."

"How old was he?"

"Maybe twenty-five. Hard to say because of the turban."

Detective Newberg **sigh**ed. "Thank you for your cooperation," she said. She handed him her card and told him if he ever heard from Armpit again to call her.

"I can go?"

She nodded.

A uniformed officer came in and **escort**ed X-Ray out of the room.

Armpit watched Detective Newberg place the photographs back in her briefcase. She shook her head, then walked out of the room.

A moment later the door to his room opened.

"So what does my expert criminal psychologist think?" She smiled, and her cheeks turned pink.

"I think he told the truth."

"You're kidding, right?"

"I mean, not at first, but then you scared him and I think he told you the truth after that."

Detective Newberg shook her head. "Now I understand how Armpit managed to sell you those **phony** tickets. You are way too **gullible**."

Armpit **shrugged**.

She smiled. "It's because you're honest. Oh, you didn't eat your pizza."

He'd lost his **appetite**.

"Well, even if X-Ray won't tell us how to find Habib, it shouldn't be all that hard to find someone whose name is Armpit. We could probably smell him a mile away."

She laughed at her own joke.

"He didn't smell bad to me," Armpit said. "I mean, that might **have nothing to do with** his name. Maybe a **wasp stung** him on the armpit or something like that."

He just had to get that in.

24

It had never felt so good to be digging and **sweat**ing in the hot sun. He didn't have to think about anything except **dirt** and **shrub**s.

Detective Newberg **end**ed **up** driving him to work, which was just as well since she drove a **normal** car and he didn't have to explain about showing up in a black-and-white.★ He did his best to **back up** what X-Ray had said. He **confirm**ed that Habib wore a turban.

X-Ray called him later and told him he'd had a nice **chat** with Debbie Newberg and that everything was cool now, but **just in case**, it might be a good idea if they stayed away from each other for a while.

Armpit didn't have the heart to tell him he'd seen and heard the whole thing. Instead, he told X-Ray about Kaira's letter.

★ **black-and-white** 경찰차를 뜻하는 은어.

"You dog! If you end up marrying that chick,★ you **owe** me at least a half a million dollars."

The phone rang the second he hung up with X-Ray.

"Okay, I just want to warn you that you're going to get a really, really **dumb** letter, so don't read it. Don't even open the envelope. Just take a **match** to it."

When he told her he'd already read it, Kaira screamed so loud he had to hold the phone away from his ear.

Then she **complain**ed about the un**reliability** of the U.S. **Postal** Service. "I thought they were supposed to be *slow!* You must think I'm a total **lamebrain**."

"I liked the letter."

"You did?"

"I liked it a lot. It made me feel good inside. Not all **goosey**, kind of ducklike."

"What?"

"Nothing. I was just trying to make a joke."

"So what do all your friends think about you having a famous rock star for a girlfriend?"

He didn't know she was his girlfriend, but he was glad she thought she was.

"I haven't really told anyone."

"You are so . . . I don't know. Other guys would be all **brag**gy about it. You're just so real. So **down-to-earth**. I feel like a big phony whenever I talk to you."

★ **chick** 젊은 여자를 뜻하는 속어.

"I don't think you're phony."

Kaira **force**d a laugh. "That's because you don't know me. I'm so **fake** I can't even tell when I'm being honest or not. Like you know when I told you to burn the letter? I was lying. I was hoping you'd read it. I just didn't want you to know I wanted that."

"I figured as much."

"You did?"

"Well, I mean, if you really wanted me to burn the letter you wouldn't have waited a few days to call me."

"You are so smart. You see right through me."

That might have been the first time anyone had ever told him he was smart.

"Okay," Kaira said, "you've got to tell me something **embarrass**ing about you now."

"Why?"

"Because I wrote an embarrassing letter to you."

"I didn't ask you to write it."

"You have to," said Kaira. "That way we'll be **even**. Otherwise I'll never be able to look at you again."

"All right," Armpit agreed. He thought a moment. "All right, you know that song '**Damsel** in **Distress**'?"

"Uh, yeah, I think I've heard of it," Kaira said **sarcastic**ally.

"Well, yeah, I know you know the song. What are the words after 'this something, this something, this dress. You would never guess . . .'—then what comes next?"

"Why?"

"Because every time I hear the song it sounds like you're singing something, but I know it can't be that."

"What does it sound like?"

"Okay, this is really embarrassing, but you asked for it. Every time I hear the song, it sounds like you're singing, 'Armpit. Save me, Armpit. A damsel in distress.' "

Kaira laughed. "'Save me, Armpit'!" she **exclaim**ed. "Why would I sing 'Save me, Armpit'? That doesn't **make sense**."

"I know!"

"I didn't even know that was your name! I didn't even know you when I recorded the song!"

"I know! I know you weren't really singing that. I already told you that."

"God, you're even worse than me. I just wrote you a dumb letter. You're **delusion**al!"

"So are you going to tell me the real words or not?"

"I didn't know there was anybody in the world named Armpit!"

"Will you **humor** me and tell me the words?"

Kaira **recite**d the words. "'These shoes, these jewels, this dress. A perfect picture of success. You would never guess . . .'" She **pause**d and said the next two words slowly and clearly. "'*I'm but* a damsel in distress. Save me. I'm but a damsel in distress.'"

"Well, that makes more sense," Armpit agreed.

"You are so funny," said Kaira. "Just hearing your voice. You don't know how much I miss you."

"Me too."

"Really?"

"Yeah, I really do. I tried not to miss you too much, because I never thought I'd ever hear from you again, but once I got your letter, and now hearing you . . . It's like your voice cuts right to my heart."

"Aw, you are so sweet. You know what we should do? We're going to be staying in San Francisco for three days this weekend. I'll be doing a show there, a show in Marin, and one in Berkeley. You should come visit me!"

"Yeah, right, I'll just hop on my private jet."

"We fly people in all the time. A guitar player gets sick or something."

"You're serious."

"I am serious. We'll **arrange** everything. A limo★ will pick you up at your house and take you to the airport."

"You're serious?"

"Three days in San Francisco. Just you and me. What do you say?"

It was **incomprehensible** to him. She **might as well** have asked him if he wanted to fly to the moon. Which was probably why he said what he said.

"Sure, why not?"

★ **limo** (= limousine) 리무진.

25

"You have to t-tell your p-parents," said Ginny.

"Why?"

"Because. They're your parents."

They were taking their daily walk.

"Think about it, Ginny," said Armpit. "Do you really think I'm going to San Francisco? Look around. Do you really think a limo is going to come driving up this street and park in our driveway?"

"Yes."

Armpit stared off in the **distance**. "San Franciso," he said.

"San Francisco," Ginny repeated.

"I'm scared of **earthquakes**," he told her.

A woman named Aileen called him on Tuesday and asked him

for his United **Airlines**★ **frequent** flyer number.✳ When he told her he didn't have one, she said United was the only airline that flew **nonstop** from Austin to San Francisco, and she suggested he **enroll** in their frequent flyer program when he got to the airport since he'd be getting double miles for flying first class.

She sounded **incredibly efficient**. She **rattled off** several **departure** and arrival times as he **struggled** to **keep up**. She suggested he take the 11:55 flight, which got into San Franciso at 1:10, because the only other nonstop would get him in at 6:21, which might make it difficult to make the eight o'clock show in Berkeley, depending on **traffic**, unless he wanted to fly into Oakland, in which case he would fly American,★ but there would be a **layover** in Dallas.

He went with her first suggestion.

"The eleven-fifty-five?"

"Whatever you said."

It wasn't until after he **hung up** that it **occur**red to him he'd miss his **economics** final. That was, if he really went.

Aileen sat at an **antique** desk looking over the hills of Santa Barbara and out to the Pacific Ocean. Unfortunately, what the hotel **offer**ed in **charm** and **serenity**, it **lack**ed in modern technology, such as in-room Internet connections. She'd had to connect her laptop to her cell phone but kept losing **reception**.

★ **United Airlines, American (Airlines)** 미국의 항공 회사.

✳ **frequent flyer number** 항공 회사의 마일리지 카드 번호.

Which meant she still hadn't booked Theodore Johnson's ticket.

She heard the **click** of her door being unlocked, and then Jerome Paisley **poke**d his large head into the room. "Have you made the **arrange**ments?"

She lazily **glance**d his way. "I just have to book the flight."

"Wait till you hear this?" he said, coming up behind her. "You won't believe it!"

"Tell me."

Jerome massaged the back of her neck as he spoke. "Fred ran a background check. The kid's got a **criminal** record. **Assault** and **battery**!★"

Aileen turned around to look at him.

"Am I a **genius** or am I a genius?"

She rose from her chair, then stood on **tiptoe** to kiss him. "You're a genius," she **whisper**ed.

"See, genius isn't all about ***intelligence***," he explained. "There are a lot of smart people in the world. Smarter than me. It's about *recognizing your* ***opportunities***. It's about letting your opportunities come to you. Sometimes all you have to do is open the door and opportunity walks right in. It takes a genius to know when to open the door."

Aileen knew a thing or two herself about recognizing opportunities. She had recognized Jerome Paisley as a weak, in**secure** man who was **constant**ly trying to **impress** everybody. She let herself be impressed.

★ **assault and battery** [법률] 폭행, 폭력 행위.

So far, with the help of Jerome, she had managed to **extract** nearly three million dollars from Kaira's trust **account**. Even he didn't know the **extent** of her **embezzle**ment.

Jerome began to **pace**. "Now's the time. Now's the time," he said, talking more to himself than to Aileen. "She'll be eighteen in two months. Now's the time to act. Opportunity is knocking. I've got no choice. Now's the time to open the door."

He was **rambling**. Aileen could hear the fear in his voice. She could see it in his eyes.

Kaira had said many times that she planned to **fire** him when she turned eighteen. If that happened, then whoever took his place would certainly discover the embezzlement. However, if, for example, somebody like Billy Boy killed Kaira before she turned eighteen, then her mother would **inherit** all her money. Jerome, her mother's husband, would continue to **oversee** all the **financial** matters.

"She's not a golden goose!★" he **declare**d. "I'm the golden goose. She'd still be singing in her church **choir** if it weren't for me. I made her who she is, and I can find someone else just as easily."

His plan was to stay with Kaira's mother for a couple of years to avoid **suspicion**, then **divorce** her and live with Aileen. But those weren't Aileen's plans. She had no **intention** of sharing her money or her life with that **self-absorbed maniac**.

Which was why in addition to needing to book a ticket for

★ **golden goose** 황금 알을 낳는 거위.

Theodore Johnson, she planned to book one for herself: first to Portland, then to Costa Rica. The name on her passport was Denise Linaria.

One thing for certain. She did not want to be anywhere near San Francisco when Theodore Johnson got there.

ꕥ

The concert that night was in an outside **amphitheater**, **nestle**d in the **foothill**s. Kaira waited on a **patio offstage**. The ocean air was cool and **foggy**. She could smell the flowers that **bloom**ed around the Santa Barbara Mission.

She couldn't believe she'd be seeing Theodore again in just three days. Aileen had booked the ticket. It almost made her like Aileen again.

More than once she had thought about telling her mother about Aileen, but she couldn't bring herself to do it. It wasn't just that she didn't want to hurt her mother. As much as she hated to **admit** it, the sad truth was that she, Kaira, *needed* El Genius. Despite all her **bluster**, deep down she knew there was no way she would ever fire him. She'd be lost without him.

Once the concert started she was able to shut out all thoughts about her mother and El Genius and just disappear into the music. Out in the open air, her voice seemed to **float** all the way up to the stars. And nobody noticed, not the band, not the audience, when this time she really did sing:

"Save me, Armpit!
A ***damsel*** *in* ***distress.****"*

26

Uncharacteristically, Jack Dunlevy wore a jacket and tie. Armpit told him he looked sharp, but Jack just grumbled something about not having enough neck room. He had to go to some kind of meeting at the mayor's office.

They were at a house where two months earlier they'd installed a sprinkler system. Now there was a leak. "It's somewhere on the right side of the front yard," his boss told him.

"My right, or the house's right?" Armpit asked.

"What?"

"I mean, is it on the right when I'm standing in the street facing the house, or when I'm standing at the front door facing the street?"

"Just find the damn leak and fix it!"

He was edgy about the meeting and his clothes made him uncomfortable. Plus the homeowner wouldn't be paying him for this, no matter what caused the leak, but he still had to pay Armpit.

He left for his meeting, and Armpit looked over the area. There was no easy way to find a leak. He would just have to dig along every inch of pipe.

And he was just about to do that when a mountain laurel★ planted near the corner of the house caught his attention. He hadn't remembered that mountain laurel being there the last time.

He realized, of course, that he'd worked at forty houses, at least, and couldn't remember every plant in every yard. Still, he had to start digging somewhere, so he started there.

It took him less than twenty minutes to find the leak. Whoever had planted the mountain laurel had cut a **gash** into the sprinkler line with a **shovel**.

He **saw**ed off a two-foot **section** of the damaged pipe, then **attach**ed a new piece. He had to let the **glue** dry before he could test it, so he was sitting in the **shade** when a car **pull**ed **up**.

He **assume**d it was someone coming to see the homeowner, so it took a moment for his brain to **register** that the guy getting out of the driver's seat was Felix and the guy in the cowboy hat was Moses.

Moses pulled a third person out of the back seat—X-Ray. X-Ray had a large **bruise** on his right cheek, and he wasn't wearing his glasses. His shirt was **rip**ped.

★ **mountain laurel** [식물] 칼미아. 철쭉과의 상록 관목.

Armpit **rose to his feet**. "Are you all right? What's going on?"

"Everything's cool," X-Ray said as Moses **shoved** him along. "They just want to talk to you."

There was something wrong with X-Ray's mouth, and he spoke with a little bit of a lisp.★

"Where are his glasses?" Armpit asked.

Moses pulled X-Ray's glasses out of his front shirt pocket, held them a moment, then dropped them on the **lawn**.

"Have you heard?" asked Felix. "Somebody's been selling **counterfeit** tickets. This lady **cop** came to talk to me about it. To me? I never sold a **phony** ticket in my life. I explain it's bad for business. Sure, I might make a quick **buck**, but then I'd never sell another ticket. See, my business is based on trust."

"I told you. She doesn't think it was you," said X-Ray.

Moses **whack**ed him on the side of his head. "And I told you to shut up," he said in his **unusual**ly high voice.

"Have you read the newspapers **lately**?" asked Felix. "The mayor's all **charged up**. Got to stop all the counterfeit ticket sales! What do you think that does to my business?"

"People trust you, Felix," said X-Ray. "You're known all around town. Every hotel **concierge** and—"

"Shut up!" said Moses.

Felix continued. "Now they're even talking about passing a law to make ticket **scalp**ing **illegal**."

★ **lisp** 's'를 'th'로 발음하는 혀짤배기소리.

"They can't do that," X-Ray said. "It's un**constitution**al."

Moses whacked him again. "Man, what does it take?" He turned back to Armpit. "How do you **put up with** him?"

"You know what the cop asks me?" Felix asked. "You want to know her number-one question? 'Where's Armpit?' That's her question. 'Where does he live? What's his phone number?' And all I'm thinking is: *Who the hell is Armpit?* But then it comes to me. I remember those two **dude**s I met at the Lonestar. I kinda liked those guys. They seemed cool. So I tell her I never heard of nobody named Armpit."

"We **appreciate** that," said X-Ray.

"Shut up!"

"But you know what happens when there's a loss of trust? People are afraid to buy tickets. **Demand** goes down. Prices drop. Way I **figure** it, Armpit, your two little phony tickets have cost me about two thousand dollars so far."

"Armpit didn't know anything about it!" said X-Ray.

Moses was about to hit X-Ray again, but Armpit took a step toward him. "Don't touch him."

"Oh, yeah?" said Moses, **challenging** him. "What are you going to do about it?"

"**Settle down**," said Felix. "Here's the thing, Armpit. I could tell **Detective** Cutie-pie★ everything I know, but how does that help me?"

"It doesn't," said X-Ray.

★ **cutie-pie** 깜찍하거나 귀여운 대상을 다정하게 부르는 말.

"It doesn't," Felix agreed. "The damage is already done. But maybe there's a way we could help each other. You help me make my money back, and even make some money for yourself while you're at it."

"What do you have in mind?" Armpit asked, his eyes on Moses.

"Kaira DeLeon's letter. I'll pay you a hundred and fifty dollars for it."

"It's not for sale," Armpit said **firm**ly as he shot a glance at X-Ray.

Felix smiled. He turned to Moses. "What do you know? Our friend X-Ray wasn't lying."

"Hey, I've never lied to you," X-Ray said. "You just got to understand where I'm coming from."

A **pickup truck** pulled up behind Felix's car.

"Look, here's the deal, Armpit. You sell me the letter or else I talk to Detective Cutie-pie. Your choice. Everybody wins, or everybody loses."

Jack Dunlevy got out of the truck. He no longer wore his jacket and tie.

"You got twenty-four hours," Felix said, then handed Armpit a business card with his phone number on it. "By the way, is your real name Habib?"

Armpit didn't answer.

The heel of Moses's boot came down on X-Ray's glasses; then he and Felix headed back to their car, crossing paths with Jack Dunlevy coming the other way.

"Sorry, man," X-Ray said. "I'm really sorry. The only reason I told him about the letter was because I was trying to explain how no one got hurt by the phony tickets."

"Yeah, well, sometimes you talk too much," said Armpit.

"I do," X-Ray agreed. "I do talk too much."

Armpit picked up X-Ray's glasses. The **frame**s were bent and a lens had **pop**ped **out**, but there was nothing that couldn't be fixed.

"Well, you just do what you think is right," X-Ray said. "Don't worry about me. If I go to jail, it's my own fault."

Jack Dunlevy came toward them. "I'm not paying you to stand around and talk to your friends," he said, but didn't sound especially angry.

"I fixed the leak," Armpit told him. "I was just waiting for it to dry so I could test it."

His boss looked around at the **relative**ly **undisturbed** lawn.

Armpit told him about the mountain laurel.

His boss smiled, then turned to X-Ray. "See, that's why I'm giving him a **raise** and a **promotion**. He's got more than a strong back. He's got a brain, too."

The meeting had been a success. Jack Dunlevy told Armpit he got the **contract** to **landscape** the performing arts center. He was going to have to **hire** a whole **bunch** of new people. And he wasn't **kid**ding about the raise and promotion. "You'll have your own **crew**. We start this weekend."

He turned back to X-Ray. "So what happened to you? Was it those guys?"

"I'm okay."

"You wouldn't like a job, would you? Six-fifty an hour?"

"Sounds good," X-Ray said, much to Armpit's surprise. "But I want to be **up-front** with you **straight off**. I've got a record."

Jack Dunlevy **consider**ed a moment. "You at Green Lake too?" he asked.

"Yes, sir. That's where I met Theodore."

Armpit almost laughed. It sounded strange to hear X-Ray call him by his real name.

"In that case I'll make it seven dollars an hour," said Armpit's boss. "You guys are the fastest diggers."

27

Armpit's economics teacher once told the class about a donkey standing exactly halfway between two **identical haystack**s. Since it had no reason to choose one haystack over the other, it just stayed in the middle until it died of hunger.

Everyone in the class **argue**d that a donkey wouldn't really do that, but that wasn't the point. Actually, Armpit couldn't remember what the point was. Like a lot of what he learned in economics, it didn't **make sense** in the real world.

But the image of that donkey remained in his head all year. He couldn't **get rid of** it. Its long ears **droop**ed and its head **hung** low as it became thinner and thinner. He wanted to scream at it. "Just pick one and go eat!"

Now he was beginning to understand what it felt like to be that donkey.

He didn't study for his economics test. He didn't call Felix. He didn't tell his parents about Kaira DeLeon inviting him to

San Francisco. He didn't tell his boss that he couldn't work this weekend.

Armpit figured that Felix would probably sell the letter on eBay.★ He'd heard about a piece of gum **chewed** by Madonna going for six thousand dollars.

Just what Kaira wanted—her **personal** letter read by millions of people over the Internet. But if he didn't sell Felix the letter, then X-Ray would go to jail. Maybe he would too. If he went to San Francisco he'd fail economics.

And so he remained, **paralyzed** by **indecision**, a donkey between two haystacks.

★ **eBay** 인터넷 경매 사이트.

28

He lay awake all Thursday night, but when he got out of bed Friday morning he had a plan. It didn't solve all his problems, but at least he'd come to a decision. He realized he couldn't do everything. He couldn't please everybody.

He called Felix, then went to school and took his speech final. It was **ridiculous**ly easy, as he knew it would be, with only **multiple** choice and true/**false** questions.

He didn't go to **economics**. There was no point. He hadn't read the last three chapters.

His feeling of regret was so strong that he actually felt pain walking away from the school building, but he'd made a decision and he knew he had to **stick** to it. He felt bad about **let**ting Jack Dunlevy **down** too. Other people **complain**ed about their bosses, but Jack had been more than **fair** with him.

But when someone like Kaira DeLeon invited you to San Francisco, how could you not go? He could hear her voice singing in his head.

Got no ***rearview mirror***
And none on either side.
Ain't no lookin' back, babe,
When I take you for a ride!

Who knew, he might never have to work again. Whether or not he **graduated** from high school wouldn't mean **a** whole **heck of** a lot.

A **horn honk**ed. He turned as the car made a sudden U-turn, then came right at him. It stopped against the curb, with its back end **sticking out** at a forty-five-degree **angle**.

Felix and Moses came out from either side.

"I want the letter now," said Felix.

"I told you Monday."

"I know what you told me. I want it today. I don't **appreciate** being **strung along**."

"I'm not stringing you along. Look, it's like you said. You talk to the police, everybody loses. You wait till Monday, everybody wins."

Moses's **fist slam**med against the side of Armpit's head, spinning him backward.

Armpit managed to keep from falling. He raised his hands with his **palm**s out. "Just wait."

Moses didn't want to wait. He came at Armpit again, but this time Armpit saw him coming. Armpit **duck**ed under the

swinging fist, then **charge**d like a **bull headfirst** into him.

Moses's cowboy hat flew off as he fell back against Felix's car, **crack**ing a headlight.

He was lucky it was the headlight and not his head.

Moses **got** back **to his feet**, **rub**bed his hands together, and smiled at Armpit.

Armpit readied himself.

Moses took one step toward him, **fake**d with his right, then slammed his left fist into Armpit's **gut**.

Armpit **double**d **over** but **fend**ed off the next **blow**, and the two of them fell to the ground and rolled into the **gutter**, fists flying as they **trade**d punches. Armpit took several blows to the head, but Moses's punches only got weaker, while his own seemed to gain power.

A horn sounded from the street, and Armpit looked up to see a long white limousine stopped in the middle of the road. "I called the police!" the driver shouted, pointing to his cell phone.

Armpit rose to his feet. He took a couple of steps backward as he watched the limo drive down the street and turn the corner.

"Just give me till Monday," he said. "You'll get the letter."

Moses pulled himself to his feet using the side mirror for support.

The cowboy hat lay on the ground, white with a brown band. Armpit, remembering X-Ray's glasses, stepped on it.

He walked the rest of the way home without once looking back over his shoulder.

The white limo was now parked in front of his house. The driver stood beside it, but when he saw Armpit, he got back inside and locked the doors.

Armpit knocked on the window.

The driver showed him the cell phone and started pushing the buttons.

"It's me! Theodore Johnson. I'm the guy you're here for. Just let me get my **stuff**."

He hurried into the house, unsure if the driver would still be there when he returned. When he saw himself in the mirror he was even more **doubtful**. He looked like a wild man. Sweat and blood **drip**ped from his face onto his **torn** clothes. Even he would cross to the other side of the street if he saw himself coming.

There was no time to shower. He took off his shirt and **splash**ed his face and upper body with cold water, then sprayed himself with Sploosh. A **knuckle** on his right hand was **bleed**ing, so he put a Band-Aid★ on it.

He put on a clean shirt and put three others in his backpack, along with a pair of long pants and some socks and underwear.

In the bottom of his sock **drawer** was Kaira's letter and the money from the ticket sales, almost a thousand dollars. He took it all, including the letter.

He went into the kitchen, and, looking out the window, he

★ **Band-Aid** 반창고의 상표명.

was a little surprised to see the limo still parked out front. He wrote a note on the **pad** next to the telephone.

Dear Mom and Dad,

I won't be back until Sunday night. It's just something I got to do. Don't worry.

T

He didn't know what else he could say. He realized he should call Jack Dunlevy, but there wasn't time and he didn't know what he'd say to him, either. He just had to hope that X-Ray would **cover** for him. He **grab**bed his backpack and went outside.

The limousine driver came around and opened the door for him. "Welcome, Mr. Johnson," he said. "Sorry I didn't realize who you were before."

"I'm just glad you're still here," Armpit said, settling into the backseat.

"There's water and a newspaper," the driver **pointed out**.

"Thanks."

The *Austin American Statesman* lay on the seat next to him, and there were two bottles of water in side cup holders. Armpit finished the first bottle before the car made it onto the highway.

In the **panel** above him were the radio and **temperature** controls. Armpit studied the **knobs**, then turned the air conditioner to MAX.★

★ max 최고, 최대. 'maximum'의 줄임말.

"I've got an **envelope** for you with your travel documents," the driver told him. "**Apparent**ly your fax machine wasn't working."

Armpit smiled.

Kaira's voice came over the radio.

*A sad circus **clown** who has hopes to **inspire***
*The love of the long-haired, blue-**spangled** **trapeze** highflyer,*
*Kicks off his **floppy** shoes and changes **attire**,*
Just like Clark Kent,★ or Tobey Maguire,✻
And goes up the circus ladder, higher and higher,
'Cause a clown is someone she could never admire,
But there ain't no net beneath the high wire.
*Nearing the top, he starts to **perspire**.*
He's climbing out of the frying pan . . .
And into the fire!

★ **Clark Kent** 영화 · 만화 캐릭터 '슈퍼맨'의 이름.
✻ **Tobey Maguire** 토비 맥과이어. 영화「스파이더맨」시리즈에서 주인공 스파이더맨을 연기한 배우.

29

There was a long line at the ticket counter, but Armpit **breezed** right past it and went to the one for first-class **passengers**, where there was almost no wait. The ticket **agent** called him Mr. Johnson.

He went through **security** without being searched, which surprised him because they stopped a middle-aged **bald** guy with glasses. Even Armpit knew he looked more dangerous than that guy did.

A couple of hours later he was flying over the Rocky Mountains and eating a caramel sundae.* The man beside him lived in San Francisco.

"You ever been in an **earthquake**?" Armpit asked.

"Lots of times. Nothing to worry about. You just **duck** under a desk or stand in a **doorway** until the shaking stops."

★ **sundae** 아이스크림 선데. 아이스크림을 넣고 시럽, 견과류, 과일 조각 등을 얹은 디저트.

Armpit had an image of himself **cower**ing under a desk with **plaster** and **brick**s **crash**ing around him, and big **gap**s in the floor opening on all sides.

The plane landed ten minutes early, at exactly one o'clock Pacific daylight time. Armpit took the escalator down to the **baggage claim**,★ where he **spot**ted a man holding a sign with THEODORE JOHNSON on it. The man had a baggage cart, but Armpit told him that all he had was his backpack, which he carried himself to the limo.

It was hot and sunny at the airport, although nothing like the **oppressive** heat of Texas, but when he arrived at the Wellington Arms Hotel in downtown San Francisco twenty-five minutes later, fog had filled the air and the **temperature** was **downright** cold. It was hard to believe this was the middle of July. He wished he'd brought a jacket.

Ginny will never believe it, he thought as he took a breath of ocean air. It was like the whole city was **air-conditioned**. There was also a freshness to the air that he didn't get in Texas, where it seemed that the same hot and **humid** air stayed in one place all summer long, becoming more **stale** and **stagnant** by the minute.

A doorman asked if he needed help with his **luggage**, but Armpit told him no thanks, showing that his backpack was all he had.

★ **baggage claim** 수화물 찾는 곳.

When he walked through the **revolving** door, it seemed like he had stepped into a palace. Once again he thought of Ginny. He wished she could see this. "Grand" and "**spectacular**." Those were the words he'd use when telling her about it. All around were giant **chandeliers** and **ornate** mirrors. "Ornate." That was another word he'd use.

A thin, **attractive** Asian woman wearing a blue pantsuit* **approach**ed him. "Mr. Johnson?"

"Yeah, that's me." She was the fourth person to call him Mr. Johnson that day.

"It's a pleasure to have you with us. I'm Nancy Young."

He shook her hand. A **brass** name tag **attach**ed to her blazer* had her name and the words VIP GUEST RELATIONS.

"Let me know if there's anything you need." She gave him an envelope with the keys to his room and minibar. "You're on the twenty-first floor. Everything's already been taken care of. Do you need a **bellman**?"

"No, I just have my backpack is all."

She explained that he was on a **restrict**ed floor and would need to use his room key in the elevator. "Would you like me to show you how that works?"

"No, that's all right." He thought about asking her what he should do in case of an earthquake but didn't want to sound like a **wimp**. The twenty-first floor was pretty high up. It didn't seem like ducking under a desk would do much good if the

---

★ **pantsuit** 상 · 하의가 한 벌로 된 여성용 의상.
✱ **blazer** 단체복으로 입는 자켓.

whole building fell over.

He looked around for the elevators, then started off in the wrong direction, but Nancy Young stopped him. "The elevators are right over there," she said.

Now that he saw them, he wondered how he had missed them **in the first place**. They were right out in the open. "Sorry, I've never been in this hotel before."

"Yes, it can be quite **confusing**," she said without even a hint of **sarcasm** in her voice.

She walked with him to the elevator, then showed him how to **insert** his room key card into the **slot** to gain **access** to the twenty-first floor.

"Enjoy your stay."

His hotel room **turn**ed **out** to be a two-room **suite**. A fruit and cheese plate had been left for him on a coffee table in his sitting area, **compliment**s of the hotel. He cut off a slice of very hard cheese and put it on a cracker. It **taste**d bitter, but he **figure**d it was supposed to taste that way. He **pop**ped a couple of red grapes into his mouth.

There were two television sets, one in each room, and he counted five telephones: two in each room and one in the bathroom. "Now, that's **class**," he said aloud when he saw the one in the bathroom, easily reachable from the toilet.

He was taking a shower, his hair full of jasmine-avocado★

★ **avocado** [식물] 아보카도. 열대 과일의 일종.

shampoo, when the phone rang. No problem. He opened the shower door and reached for the phone.

"Hello."

"You're here! Why didn't you call me?"

"I'm just getting cleaned up."

"Well, hurry. I've been waiting all day! God, I can't believe you're really here. I can't wait to see you. I'm going out of my mind!"

"Me too."

"Call me as soon as you're ready. I'm in room 2122. My name's Lisa Simpson.★"

He rinsed the soap out of his hair, brushed his teeth, and used the **complimentary** mouthwash✳ to **get rid of** the cheese taste. He put on long pants for the first time in nearly two months, then called Lisa Simpson, who said she'd meet him in the lobby.

He was on his way to the elevator when Kaira's business manager stopped him. "Welcome, you must be Theodore."

"Yes, sir."

Armpit had seen him twice before: first at the concert, then in the lobby of the Four Seasons.

"Jerome Paisley, Kaira's father." He **extend**ed his hand.

Armpit remembered Kaira saying something about him being married to her mother, but she never referred to him as

---

★ **Lisa Simpson** 미국 TV 애니메이션 'The Simpsons'의 등장인물.
✳ **mouthwash** 구강 청결제.

her father. He shook the man's hand.

"Your flight okay?"

"Yeah, it was great," Armpit said. "Thanks. I really **appreciate** you bringing me out here and everything."

The man smiled. "Happy to do it. If there's anything you need, you just let me know."

"I'm fine. Everything's really great. Thanks."

"You like baseball?"

The question caught Armpit by surprise. "I guess."

"C'mon, I want to show you something."

Armpit had no choice then but to go with Kaira's manager. He didn't want to be rude.

Jerome Paisley opened the door to his hotel room. "I'll just open the door. You walk right in," he said.

It was a strange thing to say, and he said it in a strange way, but Armpit went inside.

The suite was identical to Armpit's. Kaira's stepfather slid open a **closet** door and pulled out a baseball bat, holding it by fat end. "Take a look at this baby!"

Armpit took the bat. "Cool." He didn't know what else to say.

"See the **initial**s, B.B.?"

The letters were above the label.

"Barry Bonds,★" said Kaira's father. "Go on, take a few

★ **Barry Bonds** 배리 본즈. 미국 프로야구선수. 메이저리그 최초로 '500홈런-500도루'를 달성했다.

swings."

"That's okay," said Armpit.

"Go on, you won't break it."

Armpit took the bat, made sure he had room, then took a half swing. He felt silly.

"Feels pretty good, doesn't it?" said Jerome Paisley. "You could hit a lot of home runs with that baby."

Armpit didn't know all that much about baseball, but he was pretty sure that it wasn't the bat that hit the home runs, but the person who swung it.

"You know, I used to play pro ball," Kaira's manager told him. "Just one season in the big leagues before an injury ended my career."

One season was an **exaggeration**. Jerome Paisley played in the major leagues for just eighteen days in September, when teams are **allowed** to expand their **rosters**. The **so-called** injury was more mental than **physical**. After having been hit in the face by a **pitch**, he couldn't swing a bat without closing his eyes.

Armpit set the bat down.

"But it all **worked out** in the end, didn't it? Look at me now. Making more money than most **ballplayers**. And how long does a ballplayer's career last? Ten years if he's lucky. I'm a lot **better off** than they are, am I not?"

It took a second before Armpit realized that Jerome Paisley was expecting an answer. "Yes, sir, you're doing great," he said. "Look, I got to go. I'm supposed to meet Kaira downstairs."

"Hey, have fun. Don't **mean** to hold you up."

"Thanks. Thanks for showing me the bat." He backed out of the suite, then hurried down the hall.

Well, that was ***weird,*** he thought as he rode the elevator down to the lobby.

Kaira was waiting just outside the elevator. "It's not nice to keep a girl waiting," she said. She was all in flannel★ and **denim**, like a **lumberjack**.

Fred was standing a few steps away from her, but this time Armpit didn't let that stop him. He went right to Kaira, grabbed her, and kissed her on the lips.

She returned the kiss, letting it **linger** for several seconds. Then they smiled at each other.

"I guess it was **worth** the wait," she **whisper**ed.

★ **flannel** 플란넬. 털이 보풀보풀 일어나고 촉감이 부드러우며, 셔츠나 스커트, 양복감으로 많이 쓰는 옷감이다.

30

"You're going to **freeze**. I can't believe you didn't bring a jacket!" She held both his hands.

"It's summer. It's like a hundred degrees in Texas."

"You're not in Texas. You're here, with me."

"Well, you're pretty hot too," said Armpit.

She rolled her eyes but smiled. "Come on, we'll get you a sweatshirt★ or something at the gift shop."

She let go of one of his hands but still held the other as she led him into the **boutique**.

He began looking through the sweatshirts, trying to find one that wasn't too **cutesy**, but Kaira went straight to a **charcoal** gray wool jacket **hanging** on **display**.

"You'd look great in this!"

★ **sweatshirt** 운동 경기자가 추위를 막기 위하여 경기 전후에 입는 상의. sweat suit는 상 · 하의를 모두 일컫는 말이다.

It was pretty sharp. Armpit felt the **fabric**, which was as soft as Kaira's flannel shirt. He was about to try it on when he saw the price. Nine hundred and ninety-five dollars.

He returned to the sweatshirts even though Kaira told him not to worry about the price. "You just **charge** it to your room. The tour will pay for it."

Armpit picked out a **hood**ed red sweatshirt that said SAN FRANCISCO on it and had a picture of a **cable** car. It cost a hundred and twenty dollars, but that seemed like a bargain compared to the jacket. He charged it to his room.

Kaira called him Little Red Riding Hood★ when he put the hood up, so he put it back down. "You want to take a walk across the Golden Gate Bridge?✳" she asked.

"Sounds good."

The doorman **whistle**d for a taxi, and Kaira asked the driver if he knew the way to the Golden Gate Bridge.

"Never heard of it," the driver said, then winked at Armpit.

Armpit got in the backseat, and Kaira **snuggle**d up next to him. "You take your own **cab**," she told Fred.

She felt soft and **cuddly**, like one of Ginny's **stuffed** animals.

As they **pulled away** from the hotel, Kaira asked Armpit for a fifty-dollar bill.

Apparently she was used to being around people who carried that kind of money. For once in his life Armpit actually had

---

★ **Little Red Riding Hood** 동화 『빨간 모자』의 주인공 빨간 모자.
✳ **Golden Gate Bridge** 금문교. 샌프란시스코와 마린 카운티를 이어주는 다리.

several fifties in his wallet.

"Okay, here's the deal," she told the driver, handing him Armpit's fifty. "The guy following us is a total **doofus**. As soon as you can **ditch** him, let us out, then keep on going to the bridge."

"I like your style," the driver told her.

"Me too," said Armpit.

Kaira sang, "*I like your style/and the way you smile/just drives me wild.*"

Armpit didn't know if it was a real song or if she just made it up on the **spot**.

"You know, you got a really nice voice," the driver **remark**ed.

The cab suddenly **swerved** across three **lane**s of **traffic**. Kaira laughed as she fell across Armpit's **lap**.

The driver told them to get ready. He turned a corner, then **ease**d to a stop in front of a double-parked★ UPS✳ truck.

"Go!"

Kaira opened the door and jumped out. Armpit only had one foot on the **pavement** when the driver **hit the gas**. He **swung** the door shut and **grab**bed Kaira's hand to keep from falling.

They **crouch**ed down behind the large brown truck as the taxi with Fred in it drove right on by.

★ double-park 이중 주차를 하다.

✳ UPS (= United Parcel Service) 미국의 택배 회사.

Jerome Paisley **slip**ped the key card into the **slot** and was pleased to see the green light come on. He checked the **hallway** one last time, then opened the door to Armpit's **suite** and stepped quickly inside.

He wore a pair of latex★ gloves, the kind worn by **surgeon**s. They fit tight, like an extra **layer** of skin.

He took a quick look around the sitting area, then went into the bedroom, where Armpit's clothes were **strewn** across the floor. He picked up a **sweat-soak**ed sock, **consider**ed it a moment, then let it drop.

He entered the bathroom. Armpit's wet towel lay in a **heap** on the floor, next to the terry-cloth✻ bath**robe** the hotel had provided. The cap was off a tube of toothpaste, and some toothpaste had **leak**ed out. A hairbrush lay next to the mirror.

He picked up the hairbrush and removed a couple of **strand**s of hair that were **stuck** to the **bristle**s. He placed them in a plain white **envelope**.

A used Band-Aid, **crusted** with blood, lay on the floor next to the wastebasket. He picked it up, smiled at his fat face in the mirror, then placed the Band-Aid in the envelope as well.

He returned to the sitting area. Aileen was the one who had provided him with the extra key to Armpit's room. She also had given him two keys to Kaira's. He now placed one of them

---

★ **latex** 라텍스. 탄력 고무.
✻ **terry-cloth** 타월처럼 수분 흡수가 잘 되도록 짠 천.

between the cushions on the **couch**.

Before leaving, he took the knife from the fruit and cheese plate.

They found themselves walking through Chinatown, his arm around her shoulders, hers around his waist. **Rack**s of fruits and vegetables had been set out in front of small **grocery** stores, further **block**ing the already crowded **sidewalk**s. Trucks were double-parked up and down the street. Traffic was at a **standstill**, and people moved in and out between the cars. Yet when Armpit and Kaira stopped and kissed by the **pagoda** on Grant Avenue, it seemed to each of them like they were the only two people on the street.

They continued walking. Armpit was amazed by all the people and wondered what their lives were like. He felt like he was in a foreign country. Women **grumble**d in Chinese as they picked through vegetables and melons that he'd never seen before.

"Look at those," he said, pointing at green beans that were well over a foot long.

"I don't like **veggies**," said Kaira.

The insides of the stores seemed even more **exotic** and mysterious than the vegetables displayed on the sidewalk, but he couldn't get her to go in one with him. She had been **gross**ed out by a **string** of dead ducks hanging in a window.

"I think it's cool," said Armpit.

"That's because you're not a duck," said Kaira.

She agreed to stop at a store selling Chinese **souvenirs** because he wanted to buy something for Ginny. The silk slippers would have been perfect, but he didn't know what size to get, and Kaira **pointed out** that slippers weren't like T-shirts; they had to be an exact fit.

Going through a rack of clothes, he came across a sweatshirt that was **identical** to the one he was wearing. The price was nineteen ninety-nine.

"It's not the same," said Kaira. "It doesn't have a hood."

"That's one expensive hood," said Armpit.

"That's not the only difference," said Kaira. "Feel the fabric."

It didn't feel all that different to Armpit, but he didn't say so.

He **ended up** buying Ginny a silk scarf that showed the Golden Gate Bridge **stretching** across a background of blue sky and green ocean.

31

"God, I can breathe again," Kaira said. The crowds of people and the strong smells of Chinatown had gotten to her. "I could kill for a cup of coffee."

He believed her.

They were now in the Italian **section** of the city, which Kaira said was called North Beach, but he didn't see any sand or water. The streets were lined with Italian restaurants, cafés, bookstores, and other small shops. One shop sold nothing but old postcards.

"It's not a beach," Kaira explained. "It's just called that."

"Kind of like Camp Green Lake," said Armpit.

They went down into a **basement** coffeehouse. **Interspersed** between the tables, **vertical** wooden **beams** supported the ceiling. The wood seemed especially dark and rich, as if it had been **absorb**ing coffee for the last fifty years.

The girl behind the counter had a **teardrop tattoo** under

her left eye. Kaira ordered a double cappuccino and asked for **whipp**ed cream on top.

"The same," said Armpit. He would have felt **dumb** asking for a Coke* in a place like this.

The coffee was **serve**d in cups the size of soup bowls. The **eternal**ly crying girl **sprinkle**d powdered chocolate over the whipped cream. Kaira picked out some kind of **twist**ed **pastry** that was big enough for them to share, then took her coffee and pastry and went looking for a table.

"Nine dollars and twenty cents," said the girl behind the counter.

Armpit was surprised by how **cheerful** she sounded. He paid with a ten and left the change in the tip **jar.***

Kaira was emptying a **packet** of sugar into her coffee when he sat down next to her. The remains of another sugar packet lay in a small coffee **puddle** next to her cup.

"Isn't this place great?" she asked. "Beatniks* used to read poetry and play bongos* on that stage."

The stage was a **triangular** space in the corner, raised about a foot off the floor. It was empty now, but there were small posters **attach**ed to the beams, **advertising various** folksingers*

---

* **Coke** 코카콜라.

* **tip jar** 팁을 넣는 통.

* **beatnik** 비트족. 1950년대 전후 미국의 풍요로운 물질 환경 속에서 구식 질서에 반발해 저항적인 문화와 사고 방식을 추구했던 젊은 세대를 말한다.

* **bongos** [타악기] 봉고. 중남미의 민속악기로서, 일반 드럼보다 크기가 작으며, 지름이 다른 2개를 묶어서 하나의 악기로 사용한다. 넓적다리 사이에 끼우고 양손 손가락으로 치면서 연주한다.

* **folksinger** 민요 가수. 포크 송 가수.

and **poets** who would be performing over the next few weeks.

Armpit just hoped the beams were strong enough to hold up in an **earthquake**. If they'd been around since beatnik times, they must be strong, he thought. Either that or they were ready to break at the next little shake.

He tried to take a **sip** of his cappuccino but couldn't quite **figure out** how to do it without getting whipped cream on his nose.

"I'd like to sing on a small stage like that. No flashing lights. No backup singers. No **bloodsucking agents** or business managers. Just get up there and sing, and then **pass around a hat**. People pay what they want." Her eyes **lit** up. "You could be my guitar player!"

"That'd be great," Armpit agreed. "Except I don't know how to play the guitar."

Kaira laughed. She **tore** off a piece of the pastry, **dip**ped it in her coffee, and **tasted** it. "Oh, that is so good!" She dunked a second piece and fed it to Armpit.

The pastry was good, but her fingertips were even better.

"So, how's Ginny?"

"The same," he said. "Great."

"You're so good with her," Kaira said. "I really **admire** that. I have a hard time around **handicapped** kids."

Armpit rarely thought of Ginny as handicapped.

"Have you ever heard of the Make-A-Wish **Foundation**?" she asked him.

"Yeah, I think so."

"In a couple of weeks I'm supposed to spend the day with a nine-year-old girl dying of some disease. I was her wish!"

"That's really nice of you."

He took a sip of coffee, then wiped the whipped cream off his nose with his napkin.

"I **dread** it," said Kaira. "I know, that makes me sound like an **awful** person, but I just get **creeped out** being around someone like that. My manager says it's good **publicity**. I don't know what she wants from me! I'm just a singer. It's not like I can cure **cancer**!"

"She's not expecting you to cure her," said Armpit. "Just look her in the eye. Let her know she's real."

Kaira looked deep into Armpit's eyes.

"Just like that," he said.

She smiled and said, "You are so wonderful."

"No, I'm not," he said.

"Yeah, you really are," said Kaira.

He reached across the small table and held her hand. "There's something I got to tell you," he said.

"Oh, my gosh," Kaira said playfully. "You look so serious."

"It's just that . . ." He wasn't sure how to begin. "You know at the concert, how Ginny and I had **counterfeit** tickets?"

A man wearing a shirt and tie and one pearl earring suddenly **approach**ed the table. "You're Kaira DeLeon, aren't you?"

Kaira took a second, then **admit**ted it. "This is my friend Theodore."

The guy didn't even **glance** at Armpit. "My **niece** plays your CD all the time. *The **Fountain** of **Youth**, right*?"

"Yep," said Kaira.

"Only one of her CDs I can listen to without throwing up!"

"Uh, thanks, I guess," said Kaira.

"No, really. For **overproduce**d **commercial pap**, it's not too bad." The guy **stretch**ed his arm in front of Armpit's face and said, "I'm very **honor**ed to meet you."

Kaira shook his hand.

He handed her a napkin. "Would you mind?"

Kaira showed him her empty hands, but he gave her a pen.

She signed the napkin.

"Thanks. Thanks a lot. My niece will love it. Now will you do one for me?" he asked, handing her another napkin.

"Sorry about that," Kaira said once the guy left.

Armpit **shrug**ged.

"So what were you about to tell me?"

He wasn't sure it was the right time anymore. Everyone in the café seemed to be looking at them.

"About the concert?" Kaira **prompt**ed.

Armpit took a breath. "Okay, here's the thing. You know the letter you sent me?"

Kaira laughed. "Yeah, I think I remember it. Talk about **embarrass**ing!"

"Right. So will you write me another letter? One that's not so embarrassing?"

Kaira smiled, then **lean**ed close and **whisper**ed, "Maybe it will be more embarrassing."

"No, that's not what I meant. I mean write one sometime this weekend. You don't have to mail it. Just write it in your handwriting and give it to me."

"Why?"

"There's this guy who wants to buy it for a hundred and fifty dollars."

"*What?*"

That came out wrong. He wasn't used to drinking coffee, and it felt like his brain was racing off in different directions.

"Let me explain."

"Yeah, I think you better."

"See, I didn't get the tickets from a **scalper**. Well, **technically** I did, but I didn't buy them."

"You're not **making** any **sense**."

"See, I have this friend. And he was **scalp**ing tickets. We bought twelve tickets for your concert. I paid for the tickets, and he sold them, and we **split** the profit."

"You're a ticket scalper."

"My friend is. Was. And he's the one who gave me the **phony** tickets."

"Your friend?"

"But now there's this other guy who will tell the police unless I sell him your letter. So I was thinking if you wrote another letter that wasn't too embarrassing, I could sell him that one, and my friend won't go to jail."

"Why don't I just write you ten letters? Then you can make a thousand dollars!"

"You don't understand. It's not about money."

"No, you don't care about money. Just want to keep *your friend* out of jail."

"Right."

"So how does this *other guy* know about my letter?"

"My friend told him."

"You are unbelievable."

"You don't understand."

"Maybe you should have *your friend* explain it to me!" She stood up. "You're just another **hustler**. Anything for money."

"What do you know about money?" Armpit asked. "You don't have a **clue**. You say you want to just sing in places like this and pass around the hat. You wouldn't know how to live like that. Here, buy a jacket. Only a thousand dollars. Charge it to your room. You wouldn't have a clue."

"Oh, I don't have a clue?" asked Kaira. She stood up. "I just have one question," she said. "Who was it who kissed me? You, or *your friend?*"

She picked up her cup and **toss**ed the **content**s at him, **splatter**ing him with coffee and cream.

Several people **applaud**ed. A woman in red **leather** said, "You go, girl!"

She did just that. Right out the door.

Armpit sat there a moment, wiping himself with a napkin as he tried to figure out why Kaira thought X-Ray had kissed her.

32

It was a long walk back to the hotel. Kaira was nowhere to be seen, and he supposed she'd taken a cab. He doubted she had any cash on her, but when she got to the hotel she could probably call somebody to come down and pay the driver.

He headed back up through Chinatown. He wasn't exactly sure of the way, but he knew the **general** direction. The streets were **steep**er than he remembered, and after a while he had to take off his coffee-**stain**ed sweatshirt and tie it around his waist. He carried Ginny's present in a flat paper bag.

He wondered whether he should try to talk to Kaira when he got back to the hotel, or wait a day, or maybe just fly back to Austin. It would be pretty **weird** spending the weekend in the hotel with her hating him and everybody on the tour knowing about it. Maybe just write her a note.

He'd thought asking her to write the second letter was such a great plan, but now it just seemed so **lame**. What good would it have done? **Detective** Newberg was smart. She'd **eventually** figure out he was Armpit, whether Felix told her or not.

He had tried to take too big a step, and the **current** had **knock**ed him **off** his feet and was washing him away. All his efforts, at school and at work, were for nothing. X-Ray would most likely go to jail, and he probably would too.

For what? The **whim** of a rich and famous girl.

He had thought he'd made a real connection with her, but what did he know? It wasn't that long ago that he'd thought he made a real connection with Tatiana. The truth was, half the girls at school could have easily won his heart. It wouldn't have taken all that much; just a smile and he'd be **hook**ed.

But would he have thrown his life away for one of them, or was it just because Kaira was rich and famous? He had **mock**ed her for wanting to **charge** a thousand-dollar jacket to her room, but maybe that was the reason he came to San Francisco, to live that kind of **highfalutin** life.

No, it was more than that. At least, he thought it was more than that. He didn't know anymore. He didn't know nothing about nothing.

And he had told her she didn't have a clue! *I'm the one who's clueless.*

He took a deep breath. The cool ocean air mixed with the **exotic** smells of Chinatown. There was something special about being in a strange place, all alone in a mass of people, even if you had just **screwed up** your life, or perhaps *especially* if you had just screwed up your life.

He stopped and bought some kind of **steamed bun**, still **piping hot**, from a Chinese **vendor** who didn't speak English. The **dough** was made of rice **flour**, and it was soft and **spongy** on the outside. Inside was some of the best **roast** pork he'd ever eaten.

He was **reminded** of the speech for Wilbur the Pig. "He'll **bring about** world peace, and if he doesn't, everyone will get a ham sandwich."

*I may have **ruined** my life,* Armpit thought, *but at least I got to eat some really good Chinese food.*

Fred moved with **determination** along the **pedestrian** walkway on the Golden Gate Bridge, **oblivious** to the dirty **glances** from slow-walking tourists as he **elbowed** his way past them. His face had the look of pained **urgency**. He had never lost Kaira before.

Every walker on the bridge, every driver in a car **represented** danger. Although, really, what worried him the most wasn't some wild-eyed stranger. Sure, Theodore Johnson seemed like a good kid, but what did they know about him? Not much, except that he had a **violent criminal** history.

Fred made his way past the first tower on the bridge and was able to get a good **view** of the people up ahead. He **spied** a person wearing a red sweatshirt, but the person walking next to the red sweatshirt had on a yellow jacket and was too tall.

33

Kaira listened to *Gilligan's Island*★ in the shower through a special speaker connected to the TV. She would have to leave for the concert in a little over an hour.

Not all the **moisture** on her face came from the shower **nozzle**. Some of it came from thinking that nobody would ever like her for who she was, only for what she was.

She'd be glad when the concert started and she could **lose herself in** the songs. Singing about heartbreak and **betray**al would come easy. She'd have to **conjure** up an imaginary person again for the love songs.

Jerome Paisley knocked on the door to her **suite**, waited a moment, the **slip**ped a key card into the lock. He opened the

★ **Gilligan's Island** 미국 CBS 방송국에서 방영한 시트콤. 태평양의 미지의 섬 Gilligan에서의 모험을 그린 내용이다.

door and **stuck** his large head inside.

"Kaira," he said, but not too loudly. He held the baseball bat. His hands were sweating inside the latex gloves.

He entered and pulled the door gently shut behind him. He could hear the shower running and the sound of the television.

Kaira's suite was bigger than his, with three rooms and a working **fireplace**. It always **bug**ged him that she got the best room.

The Skipper was **yell**ing at Gilligan.

As Jerome Paisley made his way through the suite, he could feel his blood **pound**ing inside his head. His eyes **blur**red **momentarily**, and he stopped to take a breath. So far it had just been a plan, an **intellectual** exercise by El Genius, but there was a big difference between the planning and the doing.

He gathered his courage and continued into the bedroom. He **grab**bed hold of a **bedpost** to **steady** himself, then waited just outside the bathroom door. The shower was still running.

He heard a **rattling** noise, then realized that his hand was shaking so much, the bat was knocking against the wall. He hoped Kaira hadn't heard it.

Armpit was **winded** when returned to the hotel. He had always thought the hills in Austin were **steep**, but they were nothing **compare**d to where he'd just been. One of the streets was so steep the **sidewalk** had been shaped to form stairs.

The orange message lights were **blink**ing on his telephones —all five of them. He **splash**ed his face with cold water and watched the phone in the bathroom mirror blink on and off **rapid**ly.

He returned to his bedroom, sat on the **edge** of the bed, then picked up the phone. He pressed the button for messages.

"I don't hate you. I'm just sick and tired of being used by everyone. Why should you be any different? Just go ahead and sell the letter. I don't care. I really don't. Everyone else makes money off me, why not you? Besides, how can I be ***embarrassed****? I'm not a real person! I don't have feelings! I'm just a— Just go away. I never want to see you again! You're right. I don't have a* ***clue****. But neither do you."*

Well, he could have told her that.

A new voice came on.

"That was your final message. To hear the message again, press three. To save it, press six. To erase—"

Armpit **hung up**.

Kaira put on a hotel **robe**. The volume control for the bathroom speaker was to the side of the sink. She turned it down now that it didn't have to **compete** with the shower.

She towel-dried her hair. Rosemary would come fix it later. She dropped the towel on the floor, opened the bathroom door, and took one step into the bedroom.

Jerome Paisley closed his eyes as he **swung**.

The bat **carom**ed off her shoulder, then **slam**med against her **throat**.

Kaira fell against the bedpost, and before she could even

figure out what was happening, she was **struck** again, this time across her chest.

She found herself on the floor. She tried to **crawl** under the bed but was only able to **partial**ly **protect** her head. The area under the bed had been **block**ed off so guests wouldn't lose their keys and underwear.

The bat **smash**ed against the back of her neck just below the base of her **skull**.

She was only **vague**ly **aware** of what was happening as Jerome Paisley grabbed her by the **ankle** and **drag**ged her away from the safety of the bed. She saw the **eerie** image of her business manager/stepfather **split** into two people, each holding a baseball bat high above his head.

There was a noise from out in the sitting area, and then a shout.

It sounded like *the Doofus!*

Jerome turned away from Kaira and swung just as Fred **lunge**d at him. The bat **crack**ed hard against Fred's rib cage,★ but he kept coming. His hands wrapped around El Genius's thick neck as the two men fell to the ground.

Kaira watched the bat rolled across the floor and under the TV cabinet. She wanted to scream but couldn't get a breath. She tried to crawl to the telephone but couldn't raise herself off the floor.

There was an **anguish**ed **groan**; then Jerome pushed himself

---

★ rib cage 흉곽.

up to his knees, took several deep breaths, and stood up the rest of the way. He **glance**d at Kaira, then went to **retrieve** the bat.

Fred remained on the floor. Sticking into his **stomach** was the knife from Armpit's fruit and cheese plate.

The **entrance** to Kaira's hotel suite had double doors, as it was **frequent**ly used to **host** parties. Armpit was surprised to find one of the doors open. He knocked, and when there was no answer, stepped inside.

He could hear the TV coming from the bedroom. "Kaira?" he called.

Jerome **froze**. He looked down at Kaira, but she was in no **condition** to cry out.

"Kaira," Armpit called again.

No answer.

"Look, if you don't want to see me, I understand. I just came to return the letter. I'm not going to sell it. I don't want anything from you."

Jerome moved to the bedroom door, his bat ready. He really didn't want to have to kill Theodore Johnson. That would just **complicate** things.

Kaira fought to **retain conscious**ness. She tried to call out, but she had nothing left.

Armpit set the letter on the bar. "I'm just putting it right here on the bar," he said.

Good, thought Jerome Paisley. *Touch the bar.*

"Well, I'm going now," Armpit said. "Thanks for the ride. I'll never be the same again."

He waited a moment to see if his little joke might bring her out, but when it didn't, he headed to the door.

Kaira's eyes were closed, but her hand felt around under the night table.★ Her fingers wrapped around an **electrical cord**. Using every last bit of strength she had left, she pulled the cord.

The lamp came down with a **crash**.

Armpit stopped. "You all right?"

There was no answer.

"You okay, Kaira?"

He walked quickly into the **dining** area, and then on into the bedroom. "Kaira?"

He saw Kaira's stepfather just in time to raise one arm. The bat smashed against it, breaking the bone, and he **collapsed** to his knees.

El Genius swung again, but Armpit **spun** away, then pulled himself up with the help of a bedpost.

He saw Fred on the floor, and lots of blood. He didn't see Kaira.

He took several deep breaths as he backed up against the TV cabinet and readied himself for the next attack. His right arm was broken, but he was **left-handed**.

Kaira's stepfather stepped over Fred as he came at Armpit again, but just as he swung, Fred grabbed an ankle, and the bat smashed into the television set, which **exploded** in a green flash.

★ **night table** 침대 옆에 두는 침실용 탁자.

Armpit's left **fist** was still gaining **momentum** as it connected just below El Genius's nose, **floor**ing him.

Armpit was all over him, hitting him first with his fist, and then with his elbow on the backswing, again and again, until Jerome Paisley lay **motion**less.

Kaira's **hairdresser**, Rosemary, walked into the bedroom and screamed.

34

Amid the **chaos** of police, doctors, ambulance workers, TV news **crew**, Kaira's **hysterical** mother, and other people from the tour all trying to **figure out** what was happening, Armpit managed to **retrieve** Kaira's letter from the bar and **toss** it into the **fireplace**.

The last he saw of Kaira and Fred, they were being taken out on **stretcher**s. Kaira was un**conscious**. She had **passed out** right after pulling over the lamp.

Too **dizzy** to walk, Kaira's stepfather had to be held up by a couple of police officers as he was led out in **handcuffs**.

Fred was able to speak just enough to **confirm** Armpit's **innocence**, although that really wasn't much of an issue. Armpit would have thought that with him caught in the act of **beat**ing up Kaira's stepfather, everyone would have **assume**d he was the attacker, but nobody doubted his story. Maybe it was his **demeanor**, or the latex gloves on Jerome Paisley's hands, or the fact that he was the one who had shouted at Rosemary to call the police.

The next twelve hours were a **whirl**ing **blur** of **confusion**. There was nobody in **charge**. It was actually Duncan, the **bass** player, who finally called the Berkeley Auditorium and informed them that there'd be no concert. That wasn't until after eight o'clock.

Twenty thousand people were **stamp**ing their feet and shouting, "We want Kaira!" when a man came out and mistakenly announced that Kaira DeLeon had just been **murder**ed. Some people cried, while others were **desperate**ly looking for their ticket **stub**s.

Armpit was questioned four times by the police: first in Kaira's **suite**, then on the way to the **emergency room**, where his broken arm was set, then twice more at the police station. He signed a ten-page **statement**.

He didn't return to the hotel until well after midnight. In the morning he tried to find out if anyone knew anything about Kaira, but nobody did.

The people **associate**d with the tour didn't know what they were supposed to do or where they were supposed to go. Nobody knew who would pay the **enormous** hotel bill. Aileen, the woman who **normal**ly would have been in charge, couldn't be found. She had flown ahead to Portland but never checked into the hotel.

Nancy Young suggested, only **somewhat tongue-in-cheek**,

that Armpit might want to leave now, before he got **stuck** with the bill. He took a **cab** to the airport, where he was able to exchange his ticket for the next flight, but there were no first-class seats **available**. Not that he cared. He slept the whole way home, much to the **dismay** of the **passenger** sitting next to him, who kept having to **nudge** him awake.

"W-were you scared?" asked Ginny.

"It all happened so fast. I just reacted. When I think about it now, I get scared."

"Me too," said Ginny. Her eyes **moisten**ed, and she **dab**bed them with her Golden Gate Bridge scarf.

It felt **odd**ly normal to be back in Austin. "You want to sign my **cast**?" he asked Ginny.

"Yes."

It was Sunday. They were sitting in his half of the duplex. It was impossible for them to take their usual walk. The street was filled with news vans and camera crews.

Armpit's mother had had to **shoo** away a number of reporters, local and national.

"He doesn't want to be interviewed!" he'd heard her say. "Why won't you **respect** his wishes?"

It was nice to hear his mother use the word "respect" when talking about him. But then again, it wasn't every mother's son whose picture was on the front page of nearly every newspaper in the country, usually with the word "hero" somewhere in the **headline**.

Most of the **articles** had their facts wrong. According to the Austin paper, Kaira had given him a key to her room, and he had come up for a romantic **rendezvous** when he discovered she was under attack. An all-news network reported that he was in bed with Kaira when the attack **occur**red.

What must have happened, he came to realize, was that Fred had left the door to her suite open when he **rush**ed in to save her after returning from his **wild-goose chase**.

"Does Kaira know you saved her life?" asked Ginny.

"I guess somebody must have told her," Armpit said. "And it's on the news."

"She should call you."

"She will when she gets better. She's **in bad shape**."

The doorbell rang.

His mother threw up her hands. "Why won't they leave you alone?" She sounded **exasperate**d, but Armpit could tell she loved every minute of it.

"I told you people— Oh." She turned to Armpit and told him a police officer wanted to speak to him.

Detective Debbie Newberg put away her badge as she stepped inside. "Hi, Ginny."

"Hi," said Ginny.

"I need to speak to Theodore alone, if you don't mind."

If Armpit's mother was surprised by any of this, she didn't show it. Armpit **figure**d nothing surprised her anymore.

"C'mon, Ginny, let's see how many people take our picture," Armpit's mother said. She took Ginny by the hand and led her outside.

Detective Newberg joined Armpit on the sofa. "You're quite the hero," she said. Her cheeks **flush**ed pink.

Armpit **shrug**ged.

"I just wanted to let you know I've been **assign**ed to an other case. I told my **superior**s that all my **lead**s had dried up. And really, for just two **counterfeit** tickets, it isn't **worth** the resources."

"So you're not going to try to find the ticket **scalper**?"

Detective Newberg shook her head.

"I see," said Armpit, trying to sound as if the matter was of little importance to him, but a little bit of a smile **slip**ped out despite his efforts. He never had a very good **poker face**.

"Can I sign your cast?"

"Uh, sure."

He gave her the same marker Ginny had used.

Detective Newberg held his cast as she prepared to write. "So do you want it to Theodore, or to Armpit?"

"Uh . . ."

If this was a test he had just failed it.

She winked at him. "Don't worry. Like I said, case closed."

"So how'd you find out? Did Felix tell you?"

"Felix? He knew?" She seemed **genuine**ly surprised. "No, I just put two and two together and **came up with** four."

He always knew she would. "I really didn't know the tickets were counterfeit," he said.

"Oh, I figured that, too. The man who bought the real

tickets told me that X-Ray had been **reluctant** to sell them because he'd promised them to a friend. At the time I thought it was just X-Ray trying to **jack** him **around**, but then it hit me . . . you were the friend."

"X-Ray's really not a bad guy," said Armpit.

"He'd be all right if he just learned to keep his mouth shut," said Detective Newberg.

He watched her sign her name. "I always liked you," he told her. "I thought you were really cool, and smart, and I really felt bad about lying to you and everything."

Detective Newberg looked up and smiled. "No harm, no **foul**," she said, then **dot**ted the "i" in her name.

Kaira opened her eyes to see the **blur**ry image of Fred looking down at her. He was wearing a paper-thin blue hospital gown. She might have laughed if it hadn't hurt so much.

"How ya doin?" he asked her.

She tried to talk but could just barely move her mouth. Her face was heavily **bandage**d. The only **nourishment** she got was from the IV tube★ sticking into her arm.

There was something wrong with her vocal cords✻ as well, and she was only able to speak in a kind of **raspy whisper**. Fred **lean**ed close to hear her.

"Thanks for risking your life for me."

★ IV tube (= intravenous) 정맥 주사.

✻ vocal cords 성대.

Fred touched her arm. "Just doin' my job, Miss DeLeon." He winked.

He started to straighten up, but she **grab**bed his arm. There was something else she wanted to say. He had to put his ear close to her mouth to hear her.

"I'm sorry I was such a **doofus**," said Kaira.

35

Over the next two months, a lot more people signed Armpit's **cast**, most of them females who **decorate**d their names with hearts and flowers. He didn't get an F in **economics**, but an Incomplete,★ which turned into an 89 after he made up the final.

He was very lucky, and he knew it. If Jerome Paisley had succeeded in killing Kaira, Armpit would have spent the rest of his life in jail.

His **fingerprint**s were on the bat. The knife came from his room. Her room key was found in his hotel **suite**. **Trace**s of his blood and hair would be discovered in the next letter from Billy Boy. Then there was his **prior criminal** history, and the very public **argument** at the coffeehouse.

"If I was on the **jury**, even I would have **vote**d to **convict**

★ **Incomplete** 불완전 이수. 모든 학업을 완수하지 않았을 때 받는 학점.

me," he said.

"No, you'da gotten off," X-Ray **assure**d him. "How did you get the bat? You couldn't have brought it from Austin. It wouldn't fit in your backpack. And what? Did Ginny **fake** a **seizure** just so you could meet Kaira DeLeon? And you could have gotten Debbie Newberg to **investigate** for you and she would have found out about the missing money. Besides, how did your hair and blood get inside the **envelope**? What—did you cut yourself while brushing your hair, while you were writing the letter? The **frame** was too **obvious**. If you're going to frame somebody, you got to be more **subtle** about it."

"You should be a lawyer," said Ginny.

"A lawyer," said X-Ray as he **mull**ed it over. "Now you're talkin'. I'm good at the art of **verbal persuasion**."

"Otherwise known as BS,★" said Armpit.

The three of them were sitting in Ginny's room, with all her **stuffed** animals.

As it turned out, the **evidence** that would have been used to convict Theodore Johnson would now be used against Jerome Paisley to prove **premeditation**—to show he had planned to **murder** her. However, El Genius had pretty much **confess**ed to everything, so it didn't look like there would even be a **trial**.

Armpit had been a little disappointed when the San Francisco **district attorney** told him that. If there were a trial then he'd get to go back to San Francisco and see Kaira again.

★ BS (= bullshit) 실없는 것, 헛소리.

Maybe they would go to Chinatown together and eat a couple of those **steamed** pork **buns**.

He still hadn't heard from her. He thought about trying to **get in touch** with her but didn't know where or how to find her.

"You shouldn't have to call her," said X-Ray. "She should call you! Not even a thank you! She's such an **ungrateful**—" He stopped because Ginny was there.

"She's **going through** some hard times," Armpit said.

From everything he'd read in the papers, Kaira's life was a train **wreck**. That woman Aileen had stolen most of the money from the concert tour, and there were still many people who needed to be paid and ticket holders who needed to be **reimbursed**. According to the newspapers, Kaira was **broke**. Whatever money she had left was being eaten up by lawyers and **accountants**. Of course, he realized, broke for someone like her didn't mean the same as broke for someone like him.

Aileen had been **arrested** in Belize★ a few weeks earlier, but the money was never recovered. A police **detective** had discovered that Theodore Johnson's **airline** ticket was purchased over the Internet and that the same computer had also purchased a ticket to Costa Rica for someone named Denise Linaria.

Worse for Kaira than the loss of her money was the loss of her voice. The doctors said she might never be able to sing again.

★ **Belize** 벨리즈. 카리브해에 있는 나라.

Armpit looked around at Ginny's stuffed animals. Like Hooter, the owl who couldn't see, or Daisy, the dog who couldn't hear, Kaira might be a singer who couldn't sing.

36

But she did sing again.

It was in late February. Armpit was just getting out of bed when he heard her voice on the radio.

It's a lost and lonely kind of feeling,
To wake up wearing a ***disguise****.*
I lie in bed staring at the ceiling,
  I don't know who I am,
  There's little that I can
Fully ***recognize****. . . .*

Her voice sounded **fragile**, like fine crystal that might break at any moment, but each **note** was true and clear. There weren't any backup singers or **elaborate** **instrument**ation; just the gentle plinkity-plank* of a piano.

But I'm taking small steps,
'Cause I don't know where I'm going.
I'm taking small steps
And I don't know what to say.
Small steps,
Trying to ***pull myself together****,*
And maybe I'll discover
A ***clue*** *along the way. . . .*

Armpit smiled despite the **lump** in his **throat**.

Just to make it through the day and not to get hurt,
Seems about the best that I can hope.
Like coffee ***stains splattered*** *on your sweatshirt,*
There isn't any pattern.
Everything's uncertain.
It's difficult to ***cope****. . . .*

The lump in his throat turned into tears.

But I'm taking small steps,
'Cause I don't know where I'm going.
I'm taking small steps,
And I've forgotten how to play.

★ **plinkity-plank** 피아노를 띠링 띠링 치는 소리.

Small steps,
Trying to pull myself together,
And maybe I'll discover,
A clue along the way. . . .

The coffee stains were still on his sweatshirt. His mother had tried washing them out, but they were **permanent**ly set.

And if someday my small steps bring me near
you,
Please don't ***rush*** *to tell me all you feel.*
You don't have to speak for me to hear you.
If I softly sigh,
Look me in the eye
And let me know I'm real. . . .

Then we'll take small steps,
'Cause we won't know where we're going.
We'll take small steps,
And we'll have too much to say.
Small steps,
Hand in hand *we'll walk together,*
And maybe we'll discover
A clue along the way. . . .

She didn't say she would see him again, just if. The song could mean anything or nothing at all, he realized. It might just be a song that he **inspire**d, and that was nice too. More than anything, he was just glad to hear her singing again.

Anyway, he couldn't let his life **revolve** around Kaira DeLeon. He had his own set of small steps to take. 1. **Graduate** from high school. 2. Attend two years of Austin Community College.★ 3. Do well enough to **transfer** to the University of Texas. (Jack Dunlevy wanted him to **major** in **landscape architecture**, but Armpit wasn't sure he wanted to dig holes the rest of his life. He was **consider**ing studying **occupation**al **therapy**,✻ so he could help people like Ginny.) 4. Don't do anything stupid. And 5. Lose the name Armpit.

Small steps,
'Cause I don't know where I'm goin'.
Small steps,
I just take it day to day.
Small steps,
Somehow get myself together,
Then maybe I'll discover
Who I am along the way. . . .

★ **Community College** 지역 전문대학. 다양한 실용적인 학과로 이루어진 2년제 대학으로, 이곳에 진학하여 과정을 끝내고 4년제 대학(university)으로 편입하여 2년을 더 다닌 후 학위(degree)를 취득하기도 한다.

✻ **occupational therapy** [의학] 작업 요법. 적당히 가벼운 작업을 시키면서 하는 건강 회복법을 말한다.